D1646062

JOURNEY TO THE CENTRE OF THE SOUL

Withdrawn from Stock
Dublin City Public Libraries

Leabharlann na Cúirte
Cabra Library
Tel: 8691414

The Bible Reading Fellowship
15 The Chambers, Vineyard
Abingdon OX14 3FE
brf.org.uk

The Bible Reading Fellowship (BRF) is a Registered Charity (233280)

ISBN 978 0 85746 582 5
First published 2017
10 9 8 7 6 5 4 3 2 1 0
All rights reserved

Text © Andrew D. Mayes 2017
This edition © The Bible Reading Fellowship 2017
Cover image © Thinkstock

The author asserts the moral right to be identified as the author of this work

Acknowledgements
Unless otherwise stated, scripture quotations are from The New Revised Standard
Version of the Bible, Anglicised edition, copyright © 1989, 1995 by the Division of
Christian Education of the National Council of the Churches of Christ in the United
States of America. Used by permission. All rights reserved. • Scripture quotations
from The Revised Standard Version of the Bible, copyright © 1946, 1952, 1971 by
the Division of Christian Education of the National Council of the Churches of Christ
in the United States of America. Used by permission. All rights reserved. • Scripture
quotations taken from The Holy Bible, New International Version (Anglicised edition)
copyright © 1979, 1984, 2011 by Biblica. Used by permission of Hodder & Stoughton
Publishers, a Hachette UK company. All rights reserved. 'NIV' is a registered trademark
of Biblica. UK trademark number 1448790. • The New Jerusalem Bible © 1985 by
Darton, Longman & Todd Ltd and Doubleday, a division of Bantam Doubleday Dell
Publishing Group, Inc. • The Jerusalem Bible © 1966, 1967, 1968 by Darton, Longman
& Todd Ltd and Doubleday & Company, Inc. • Scripture quotations taken from the
New King James Version of the Bible copyright © 1979, 1980, 1982 by Thomas Nelson,
Inc. All rights reserved. • Scripture quotations taken from the Holy Bible, English
Standard Version, published by HarperCollins Publishers, © 2001 Crossway Bibles,
a division of Good News Publishers. Used by permission. All rights reserved.

Every effort has been made to trace and contact copyright owners for material used
in this resource. We apologise for any inadvertent omissions or errors, and would
ask those concerned to contact us so that full acknowledgement can be made in
the future.

A catalogue record for this book is available from the British Library

Printed and bound by CPI Group (UK) Ltd, Croydon CR0 4YY

JOURNEY TO THE CENTRE OF THE SOUL

A handbook for explorers

Andrew D. Mayes

Contents

Introduction

This book is a summons to a spiritual adventure, an odyssey of the soul. Its aim is to invigorate and inspire a search for something deeper in the spiritual life, and as a handbook it provides references to trusted guides that will support and nourish us as we progress on a journey of discovery. We will mine the rich seams of Christian spirituality, risk the depths, face the darkness and make astonishing, transformative discoveries. This is a book for the curious, for the inquisitive—for people who sense that there is much more to find in their spiritual quest.

In two earlier books, I have explored the spiritual life through the imagery of the visible landscape. In *Holy Land? Challenging questions from the biblical landscape* I led the explorer across the terrain of the Holy Land, which I had got to know well when working as course director at St George's College, Jerusalem, and through my ongoing ministry in regularly leading pilgrimages. There we explored the mountains, rivers, gardens, deserts and ocean and allowed the physicality of the land to throw at us vital questions and raise thorny issues in spirituality. In *Beyond the Edge: Spiritual transitions for adventurous souls* we followed Jesus into liminal spaces across the land, venturing to the coastlands, entering 'no-go areas', wading across the Jordan—all of which led us to unpack the theme of crossing boundaries in order to experience at once a radical letting-go and a startling rediscovery of the spiritual life. But now it is time to leave the surface terrain of the Holy Land and to venture underground.

This book explores the spiritual life through the extended metaphor of underground spirituality. It aims to be a handbook for explorers of the spiritual life—a guide to the interior spaces of the soul. It suggests an itinerary for explorers. Like complex cave systems, Christian spirituality can seem bewildering, disorientating—it is easy to get lost! So here I offer a guide and a pathway underground. The

Leabharlanna Poibli Chathair Bhaile Átha Cliath

Dublin City Public Libraries

subterranean world provides a range of rich imagery which helps us to discover essential resources, challenges and hidden treasures of the spiritual life.

Thus the starting point for our reflections here is the subterranean landscape itself, which becomes a catalyst for thinking about a range of issues which are both urgent and abiding. Each chapter explores a theme which is suggested by the underground features of the Holy Land. This approach is inspired by the prophetic and metaphorical approach to creation that we see in the scriptures. Topography suggests typology. The Psalms delight in the symbolism of water, rock, mountain and wind (Psalms 1, 18). Every prophet of the land exults in vivid images from the hills: the very terrain speaks the message. Isaiah cries out: 'Every valley shall be lifted up, and every mountain and hill be made low' (40:4). Hosea sees climate and field as bespeaking God: 'Sow for yourselves righteousness; reap steadfast love; break up your fallow ground; for it is time to seek the Lord, that he may come and rain righteousness upon you' (Hosea 10:12). The prophets draw from the land powerful metaphors for salvation and judgement, and the contours of the terrain become a symbolic universe. Jesus himself reveals a deeply contemplative and sacramental approach to the land, the secrets of the kingdom revealing themselves through parables of rock, mountain, field and sea (Matthew 13; Mark 11:23). The very topography poses its own questions to us that will help us as we traverse the terrain of our own spiritual journey. Physicality points to spirituality: here we explore the inner reaches of the spiritual life through imagery given to us by geography, geomorphology and geology!

The subterranean world is out of view, but beneath our feet. It is close by, but often hard to access. It is a mysterious and intriguing world of secrets and hiddenness. But caves can be dangerous places too: hypothermia, slipping, flooding, falling rocks and physical exhaustion prove to be recurrent risks for explorers. Cavers need essential equipment and clothing to sustain them and to protect them from abrasion. They need to be both courageous and sensitive—

determined, possessing stamina, but also able to tread lightly and touch softly within a fragile environment. So too the reader of this book will need to be prepared for a tough but rewarding journey into the spiritual world. Spiritual explorers will need great reserves of openness and a zest, a craving, for discoveries which might turn out to delight or unsettle, to cheer or unnerve. And just as cavers generally work better in a team, where they can look out for one another, so this resource can be well used in a group, as a tool for navigating one's way through the season of Lent, or at any time in the year.

A spirituality of descent

Onwards and upwards? Paul writes about 'the upward call of God in Christ Jesus' (Philippians 3:14, RSV), and in the history of Christian spirituality the metaphor of ascent prevails: the image of going up to God. The way to God seems to be up, up, up. Influenced by Platonic ideas in the fourth century, Gregory of Nyssa uses the climbing of mountains as a model of Christian perfection in his *Life of Moses*. Writing at the monastery at Mount Sinai, the abbot John Climacus (579–649) suggests that the virtues form 30 rungs on the *Ladder of Divine Ascent*. St Bonaventure writes of the 'mind's ascent to God' in his work *The Journey of the Mind into God*. Even John of the Cross in his masterpiece *The Ascent of Mount Carmel* uses this model of going up to God and leaving worldly things behind.[1] Ascent resonates with the modern desire for self-advancement and the seeking of promotion, 'going up the ladder', acquiring ever greater power and status. It encourages us to think in terms of hierarchy. It suggests that one must renounce the world and get away from it in order to find God.

However, our God is a descending God. Paul celebrates the *kenosis* of the Word, which leads to his welcome in the underworld (Philippians 2). The writer of Ephesians has a big question:

... each of us was given grace according to the measure of Christ's gift. Therefore, it is said, 'When he ascended on high

he made captivity itself a captive; he gave gifts to his people.'
(When it says, 'He ascended', what does it mean but that he had
also descended into the lower parts of the earth? ...)
EPHESIANS 4:7–9

Cosby writes of the descending God: 'If God is going down and we
are going up, it is obvious that we are going in different directions...
We will be evading God and missing the whole purpose of our
existence.'[2] Paul Tillich in his ground-breaking study *The Shaking of
the Foundations* invites us to rediscover the metaphor of the depths
of God:

> Most of our life continues on the surface. We are enslaved by
> the routine of our daily lives... We are in constant motion and
> never stop to plunge into the depth. We talk and talk and never
> listen to the voices speaking to our depth and from our depth...
> It is comfortable to live on the surface... It is painful to break
> away from it and to descend into an unknown ground.[3]

We are summoned to quit superficial living and risk a descent into
the depths, where we may find God and in the process rediscover
ourselves. As Richard Foster put it: 'Superficiality is the curse of
our age... The desperate need today is not for a greater number of
intelligent people, or gifted people, but for deep people.'[4]

Christians living in places of uncertainty and danger have reminded
us:

> There is no ready-made path in spirituality, even when we
> follow masters and schools, ancient and modern... there is
> no ready-made path, but Jesus is the Way... there is no need
> to wait for maps to replace our spirituality or to stop us from
> creatively exploring new heights or greater depths... our
> spirituality is an adventure into the unknown, a struggle with
> all the risks, the greatest throw of our freedom; it is both the
> meaning of and the quest for our being.[5]

The inviting caves of the Holy Land

In the Holy Land there are 45,000 caves! In Jerusalem the Hebrew University's Department of Geography has a dedicated Cave Research Unit. One of the things that strikes pilgrims to the Holy Land is the frequency with which they are required to go down into caves. Many of the holy places are, in fact, caves. The pilgrim descends underground into sacred grottos and caverns, and, in the subterranean mystery, finds God. These hidden chambers in the bowels of the earth turn out to be liminal places, thresholds of the divine, loci of theophany.

There are awesome caves associated with the Old Testament: the first to be mentioned in the Bible (Genesis 23) is the Cave of Machpelah, the burial place of Abraham and Sarah; today, this is below the great Herodian building at Hebron, which can be entered either at the Muslim side as a mosque or at the Jewish side as an adjoining synagogue. Sinai preserves the memory of Moses in the cave: to him God says: 'while my glory passes by I will put you in a cleft of the rock' (Exodus 33:22). At Sinai we recall how Elijah fled and hid in a cave on Horeb when he was in a state of fear and stress. Here God questions him: 'What are you doing here, Elijah?' (1 Kings 19:9, 13). There is also the Cave of Elijah at the foot of Mount Carmel. The Cave of Zedekiah near the Damascus Gate in Jerusalem is the largest man-made cave in the land, extending 230 metres under the Old City, and served as a quarry for Herod's rebuilding of the Second Temple. The mysterious caves of Qumran, in marl canyons overlooking the Dead Sea, held for almost 2000 years the precious documents of the Essenes, rediscovered in 1947. In the Islamic tradition, a mysterious cave below the great stony outcrop sheltered by the Dome of the Rock in Jerusalem is known as 'the well of souls', while we recall that it was after three years' solitude in the Cave of Hira near Mecca that Muhammad received the revelations of the Qur'an.

There are caves bound up with the New Testament story. The traditional birthplace of John the Baptist is found in the cave of Ein

Karem, while the domestic cave of Mary's House in Nazareth is now preserved under the largest church in the Middle East, the Basilica of the Annunciation. Around the Mount of Olives there are caves preserving special memories: the cave of Eleona where Constantine built a basilica to celebrate the teaching of Jesus, known as the Pater Noster site today; the grotto at the foot of the Mount of Olives in Gethsemane where Jesus often taught. Nearby, one descends over 80 steps from the Kidron Valley to the Tomb of Mary, a cavernous underground church which contains her empty sepulchre. The most important cave for Christians is the cave of Christ's burial and resurrection, parts of which are preserved in the *edicule* or 'little house' in the Church of the Resurrection, known as the Holy Sepulchre.[6]

Early Christian writers began to glimpse the symbolism of the caves. Eusebius of Caesarea notices a triad of 'mystical caves' which testify to three cardinal points of the then newly written Creed of Nicea: 'He was incarnate… He was crucified… He ascended…'

> In the same region, Constantine recovered three sites for three mystical caves and enhanced them with opulent structures. On the cave of the first theophany [Bethlehem] he conferred appropriate marks of honour; at the one where the ultimate ascension occurred [Mount of Olives] he consecrated a memorial on the mountain ridge; between these, at the scene of the great struggle [Calvary and tomb of Christ], the sign of salvation and victory.[7]

In this book, such caves in the sacred landscape of the Holy Land become starting points or entry points for a spiritual quest.

Joining a tradition of explorers

Throughout literature the underground world fascinates and captivates the imagination. It evokes a sense of mystery and excites both fear and hope. Caves and subterranean passages become archetypal images, summoning us, at the same time, to make astonishing and life-changing discoveries, and also to confront our deepest anxieties and darkest corners. In the world of myth and legend, secret passageways lead to an underworld, where it becomes possible to make contact with unseen powers and forces. In popular legend, caves house gnomes, spirits, dragons and forgotten undiscovered treasure. In Greek mythology, heroes such as Hercules, Theseus, Orpheus and Odysseus make their courageous *katabasis*, a journey down to the underworld. Throughout mythology heroes and heroines, even gods and goddesses, have to descend to the nether regions in order to attain healing and salvation, or to obtain a vital piece of knowledge. The tale is told of Persephone, niece of Zeus, who delighted in living on the surface amid nature but very reluctantly entered the underworld. A great chasm opened up before her, a vast crack in the surface of the earth, and in great fear Persephone made her descent. She came to enjoy the world below, discovering untold treasures, and brought solace to lonely Hades, returning to the surface for half of the year to usher in a new springtime for the earth. Every autumn as the leaves fall, Persephone returns, willingly, to the underworld, a place that is no longer forbidding but, for part of the year, her home.

In the myth behind Wagner's *Ring*, the dwarf Andvari lived in a cave where he kept his treasure. This treasure, including the Ring itself, was stolen by the deceitful god Loki, but then cursed with destructive powers by Andvari. In Wagner's operas caves are places of struggle, conflict and paradox. Humanity's true colours are revealed underground; here, goodness and envy, kindness and violence compete.

In Tolkien's *The Two Towers* Gimli celebrates the beauty of the Glittering Caves, the cave system located behind the Deeping Wall of Helm's Deep: 'Immeasurable halls, filled with an everlasting music of water that tinkles into pools, as fair as Kheled-Zaram in the starlight.' The Glittering Caves was an immense, ore-filled cave system that extended deep down into the White Mountains for many miles and consisted of many different paths, tunnels and chambers.[8] A sense of trepidation, exhilaration and anticipation builds as Richard Church's 1950 novel *The Cave* takes a group of young people deeper into the recesses of the earth. More recently the blockbusting movies celebrating Harry Potter's journeys often feature mysterious caves and underground adventures.

Jules Verne's 1864 classic odyssey *Journey to the Centre of the Earth* tells the epic account of the exploration of the underworld, a quest to discover the sources of life. The four key characters resonate with our experience as spiritual searchers, and we can identify with them in different ways. Professor Otto Lidenbrock, adventurous, determined, single-minded and impatient to make progress, is complemented by his nephew Axel, who is cautious, wary and hesitant. Grauben, Otto's goddaughter, is a gentle, beautiful soul, inquisitive and curious. Hans becomes their resourceful and imperturbable guide. In their quest, they face many dangers and risks, including monsters, storms and rock falls. In a journey they cannot predict, they experience both fearful encounters and astonishing discoveries.

Using this book

The book is designed to be used by both individuals and groups. Questions at the end of each chapter are provided to stimulate personal reflection and group discussion. Three readerships are in mind. First, it is for Christians who are longing for movement and progress in their spiritual lives. Second, it is for those who support others on their spiritual journey: those who serve as spiritual directors, soul friends or accompaniers. Third, it is for seekers, for those wanting to discover for themselves the astonishing riches of the Christian tradition. The book will open the user to a wide variety of spiritual resources that will inspire the spiritual journey. It can be used either alone or in house groups. It is recommended that both individuals and course participants keep a journal or notebook, in which to note and reflect on the transitions taking place in themselves as they undertake this life-changing journey.

1

Reading the geology of the soul: your spiritual history

The journey begins! How do you feel about becoming an explorer of the inner spaces? A mixture of anticipation blending with hope, exhilaration fighting apprehension? In this chapter we begin to read the geology of the soul: we discover and celebrate something of our unique make-up and identify the influences which have formed us thus far. It is time to see what lies beneath the surface, beneath our feet...

The landscape of the Holy Land summons us to this adventure of discovery. It is marked by vivid contrasts. The very shape of the land has been formed by grating movements along fault lines, seismic shifts and clashes between tectonic plates in the Great Rift Valley of the Jordan: here, different sorts of masses meet and interact, in more than one sense. Here, where the desert and the sea face each other, where the bleak Dead Sea in the lowest place on earth is linked to the teeming and life-giving Sea of Galilee, where wilderness and fertility lie side by side, is a land of paradoxes and deeply challenging questions.

To the north, the Galilee region has been defined by earthquakes and volcanic activity, and black basalt rocks, spewed out from the depths, are to be found everywhere.[1] A mountain range, running north to south through the centre of the region, exposes limestones and sandstones of the Cretaceous period. The Judean hills form the spine of the country, and Jerusalem sits on the top of this ridge. It was created by the massive land movements generated by the Rift Valley fault where the African tectonic plate confronts the Arabian.

Here the Jordan River flows down into the Dead Sea, the world's lowest water mass, lying in a *graben* (ditch) caused by the breaking open of the earth's crust over millennia.

To the south, in the Negev desert, is found the Ramon crater. This is not actually an impact crater from a meteor nor a recess formed by volcanic eruption, but rather is the world's largest crater, or *makhtesh*, created by the unrelenting processes of differential erosion. The hard outer layer of rock, undermined by the erosion of softer rocks below, collapsed under its own weight. As the crater deepened, more layers of ancient rock were exposed, with rocks at the bottom of the crater being up to 200 million years old. Today, the crater is 500 metres deep and reveals a diversity of rock strata, including stunning red and yellow colours and forms.

Spiritual formation

In our spiritual journey, we look to creation for descriptors of the inner, spiritual landscape—what Gerard Manley Hopkins called the *inscape*, the unique characteristics of the soul. Each of us has personal histories, hidden histories, the story of our soul. Our lives might be read like strata in rock.

The model of Christian formation has in recent years become a key way by which we can look at the influences that shape our spiritual lives. Jeremiah's image of the Potter working on the clay (18:1–6) reminds us that God not only makes us of the dust of the earth, he wants to shape and refashion us. God longs to do wonderful things with the raw material of a human life yielded to his hands. Spiritual formation is a process by which a person gets reshaped. The metaphor of formation is drawn from the natural world, speaking of a creative process at work in the landscape, both physical and spiritual. The language of formation implies that at the heart of spirituality is the raw material of a person's life, on which God acts in a creative way. Most of all, the language of formation communicates the need for us to undergo a series of changes in our inner life, an evolution. It implies a process of change. Robert Mulholland puts it succinctly: 'Spiritual formation is the experience of being shaped by God towards wholeness.'[2] Let's unpack four dimensions.

1   Spiritual formation recognises ongoing creation

Spiritual formation attests to God's ever-creative process of shaping our lives. We become caught up in God's awesome creativity, first celebrated in the hymn to creation:

> In the beginning when God created the heavens and the earth, the earth was a formless void and darkness covered the face of the deep, while a wind from God swept over the face of the waters… And God said, 'Let the waters under the sky be gathered together into one place, and let the dry land appear.' And it was so. God called the dry land Earth… And God saw that it was good.
>
> GENESIS 1:1–2, 9–10

Indeed, the language of formation evokes the second account of creation: 'the Lord God formed man from the dust of the ground, and breathed into his nostrils the breath of life; and the man became a living being' (Genesis 2:7). It recalls the language of the Psalms. Psalm 139:14–15 wonders at God's secret moulding of the person in the womb:

> I praise you, for I am fearfully and wonderfully made.
>   Wonderful are your works;
> that I know very well.
>   My frame was not hidden from you,
> when I was being made in secret,
>   intricately woven in the depths of the earth.

Psalm 119:73 links formation and learning: 'Your hands have made and fashioned me; give me understanding that I may learn your commandments.' Psalm 33:15 talks about God forming the inner person: 'he who fashions the hearts of them all'. God has a plan and design for each of us. He wants to do something beautiful in each of us, and enable us to reach our full potential in Christ. In prayer we detect the movements of the Creator Spirit. We dare to ask the question, 'What is God doing in my life?' We seek to discern and celebrate how we are growing, evolving, emerging into, as Paul put it, 'God's work of art' (Ephesians 2:10, JB). God is ever-creative:

> Do not remember the former things,
>   or consider the things of old.
> I am about to do a new thing;
>   now it springs forth, do you not perceive it?
> ISAIAH 43:18–19

We seek to discern and celebrate God's creativity in our life, so that we can tentatively name what God is doing in us.

2 Spiritual formation discovers vocation

In Isaiah's Servant Songs the language of formation is often used in partnership with that of vocation: 'But now thus says the Lord… he who formed you… I have called you by name, you are mine'; 'the people whom I formed for myself so that they might declare my praise' (Isaiah 43:1, 21). A similar link is found in God's words to Jeremiah: 'Before I formed you in the womb I knew you, and before you were born I consecrated you; I appointed you a prophet to the nations' (Jeremiah 1:5).

Christian vocation, of course, springs from baptism. As Christ received at the Jordan the affirmation 'You are my beloved Son', so in baptism God establishes our true identity as his beloved sons and daughters. Spiritual formation is alert to the uniqueness of each person and attentive to questions of personal identity: Who am I? What am I becoming? What is God calling me to be? Spiritual formation encourages us to see vocation in dynamic, not static terms, as something evolving, deepening, growing, not as a given 'once for all'. We recognise signs of a vocation unfolding in the journey from baptism to heaven. We recognise our hidden gifts. We move towards total surrender to God and to the discovery within ourselves of gifts or talents that perhaps lie latent or unfulfilled. We get in touch with our destiny.

3 Spiritual formation encourages integration

We live in a fragmenting world. Even within ourselves, we find ourselves pulled apart, caught up in a multiplicity of tasks, with so little time… caught between the commitment to help build Christian community and the call to solitude; pulled between the 'desert' and the 'city'; falling between ideals of holiness and the reality of our fragility.

We often experience a dichotomy in our lives between solitude and engagement, between action and contemplation. We too often divide things up or compartmentalise things, setting things in a needless opposition: prayer versus politics; sacred versus secular; Church versus world; time versus eternity; the body versus the soul. We find it very difficult to get in balance the 'doing' and the 'being'. Stresses and strains can be formative, for good or ill.

The idea of spiritual formation emphasises that in prayer God wants to heal our dividedness, restore our unity, renew our wholeness in Christ. We need to be on the lookout both for signs of fragmentation, inner conflict and tension, and for signs of integration, evidences of things coming together, like the interweaving of strands in a Celtic design.

We need to be attentive to the overlap and interpenetration of different aspects of Christian formation. Sometimes three dimensions are identified: *human formation*—our heart, our personal relationships, our work, our emotions, our sexuality; *intellectual formation*—our mind, the issues we grapple with; *pastoral formation*—our ministry as Christians. Such elements continually overlap and one will affect the other. Spiritual formation invites us to be attentive to the impact of our prayer on our lifestyle and our lifestyle's impact on prayer. It encourages us to explore the links between the way we pray and the way we live—to make connections between our experience in prayer and what happens to us in the world.

So, formation is based on the central Christian truth of the incarnation—God taking on our human flesh and blood on earth. The incarnation abolishes for ever and unites the great divides between body and soul, the physical and the spiritual, heaven and earth. Spiritual formation focuses on what might, in prayer, contribute to the healing of our dividedness and be awake to potential barriers to our wholeness.

4 Spiritual formation celebrates transformation

Paul emphasises our call to be transformed into Christ: 'Do not be conformed to this world, but be transformed by the renewal of your mind' (Romans 12:2, ESV). In another place he puts it: 'Beholding the glory of the Lord, we are being transformed—into the same image from one degree of glory to another. For this comes from the Lord who is the Spirit' (2 Corinthians 3:18, ESV). The Greek word Paul uses, *metamorphosis*, denotes a process of profound change.

What changes might we seek? What transformations or movements are we longing for? This might include growing awareness of God and self; 'desolations and consolations' in the Ignatian perspective; fresh realisations of how loved we are. The key transformation is growth into Christlikeness, closer resemblance to Christ, increasing identification with Christ, fulfilling our baptism. Spiritual formation is not a narcissistic, individualistic process of self-discovery. It is the process by which we become more fully conformed and united to Christ our risen Lord.

This work of transformation is essentially paschal, a walking in the way of the cross and in the way of resurrection. It requires a dying and rising, a letting go and letting God. It may well be a costly and painful process, involving a tearing down before a building up... until we can say with Paul: 'It is no longer I who live, but it is Christ who lives in me' (Galatians 2:20). We are caught up in the divine–human synergy: we become partners with God the Holy Spirit as, through prayer, he shapes us all into the people he wants us to be.

Reading the geology of the soul

Reflecting on different rock types, and the pressures they have been subject to, gives us an opportunity to take stock of our own spiritual formation, to use the metaphor. As we examine these now, bear in mind these questions: What are my defining characteristics? What has contributed to my make-up, my composition—the way I am? What have been the formative experiences and influences in my life? When have I been reshaped? Am I aware of any resistances to God, like hard rock difficult to break down?

Formed by fire

Igneous rock (derived from the Latin *ignis* meaning 'fire') forms through the cooling of molten magma or lava. This magma may be derived from partial melts of pre-existing rocks in either the earth's mantle or crust. Typically, the melting of rocks is caused by an increase in temperature, a decrease in pressure, or a change in composition. Rocks like granite result when magma cools and crystallises slowly within the earth's crust. Rocks like basalt come from magma reaching the surface as lava. Precious ores containing minerals and gold may be located here.

Fire denotes the mysterious and energising divine presence of a theophany: the burning bush that calls Moses to his liberating vocation (Exodus 3:2) and the awesome appearance of God on top of Mount Sinai: 'Now Mount Sinai was wrapped in smoke because the Lord had descended on it in fire. The smoke of it went up like the smoke of a kiln, and the whole mountain trembled greatly' (Exodus 19:18, ESV). The divine fire falls on Elijah's sacrifice on top of Mount Carmel (1 Kings 18:38), consuming the offering. But the fire of the Old Testament is not only an outer visible conflagration. Jeremiah speaks of an inner flame, a divine compulsion: 'If I say, "I will not mention him, or speak any more in his name", there is in my heart as it were a burning fire shut up in my bones, and I am weary with holding it in, and I cannot' (Jeremiah 20:9, ESV).

Shockingly, Jesus cries out in the Gospel: 'I came to bring fire to the earth, and how I wish it were already kindled!' (Luke 12:49). The writer to the Hebrews warns us: 'our God is a consuming fire' (12:29). Fire often symbolises the Holy Spirit; Luke describes his advent in these terms: 'Divided tongues, as of fire, appeared among them, and a tongue rested on each of them' (Acts 2:3). Paul exhorts the Romans (12:11, RSV) to 'be aglow with the Spirit'. To Timothy he writes: 'For this reason I remind you to rekindle the gift of God that is within you through the laying on of my hands' (2 Timothy 1:6).

Two 14th-century writers in particular delight in the imagery of fire. The English mystic Richard Rolle (1300–49) opens his treatise *The Fire of Love* with the arresting words:

> I cannot tell you how surprised I was the first time I felt my heart begin to warm. It was a real warmth too, not imaginary, and it felt as if it were actually on fire… But once I realized that it came entirely from within, that this fire of love had no cause, material or sinful, but was the gift of my Maker, I was absolutely delighted.[3]

Rolle extols, with unbridled enthusiasm, the affective dimensions of Christian spirituality: he also describes the experience of God in terms of music, sweetness and light.[4]

The Italian seer Catherine of Siena (1347–80) writes of the imagery of fire in a very powerful way:

> You know the only thing that can bind a person is a bond; the only way to become one with the fire is to throw oneself into it that not a bit of oneself remains outside it… Once we are in its embrace, the fire of divine charity does to our soul what physical fire does; it warms us, enlightens us, changes us into itself. Oh gentle and fascinating fire! You warm and you can drive out all the cold of vice and sin and self-centeredness! This heat so warms and enkindles the dry wood of our will that it bursts into flame and swells in tender loving desires, loving what God loves and hating what God hates. And I tell you, once we see ourselves so boundlessly loved, and see how the slain lamb has given himself on the wood of the cross, the fire floods us with light, leaving no room for darkness. So enlightened by that venerable fire, our understanding expands and opens wide. For the light from the fire lets us see that everything (except sin and vice) comes from God… Once your understanding has received the light from the fire as I've described, the fire transforms you into itself and you become one with the fire… How truly then we can say that he is a fire who warms and enlightens and transforms us into himself![5]

In the 16th century John of the Cross (1542–91) delights in the image of a human log becoming radiant in the divine flame: 'We can compare the soul in… this state of transformation of love to the log of wood that is ever immersed in fire, and the acts of this soul to the flame that blazes up from the fire of love. The more intense the fire of union, the more vehemently does this fire burst into flames.' It is a blending of fires human and divine, for John notes: 'Such is the activity of the Holy Spirit in the soul transformed by love: the interior acts he produces shoot up flames, for they are acts of inflamed love, in which the will of the soul united with that flame, made one with it, loves most sublimely.'

The divine flame cauterises the soul, and at once heals and pains—a divine wounding:

> *O living flame of love*
> *That tenderly wounds my soul*
> *In its deepest centre!*[6]

In our own time, this archetypal language continues to resonate in our souls: Graham Kendrick prays: 'Blaze, Spirit blaze, Set our hearts on fire!' David Evans sings: 'He burns with holy fire, with splendour he is crowned.' So what does it mean?

The divine fire first denotes God's purifying activity within us: 'For he is like a refiner's fire... he will sit as a refiner and purifier of silver, and he will purify the descendants of Levi and refine them like gold and silver, until they present offerings to the Lord in righteousness' (Malachi 3:2–3). Isaiah experiences a burning coal on his lips and in the same moment recognises God's call: '"Whom shall I send, and who will go for us?" And I said, "Here am I; send me!"' (Isaiah 6:8). John the Baptist speaks of God's fire of judgement: 'the chaff he will burn with unquenchable fire' (Matthew 3:12).

A second theme is the empowering, energising presence of God in us. The divine fire, kindled within us, illuminates our way and causes us to shine out with inextinguishable love—we are called to irradiate divine love, to be incandescent.

As the Orthodox Liturgy for Easter puts it:

> Now are all things filled with light;
> Heaven and earth, and the nethermost regions of the earth![7]

In a memorable episode from the Desert Fathers we learn the soul's true potential:

Abba Lot went to see Abba Joseph and said to him, 'Abba, as far as I can I say my little office, I fast a little, I pray and meditate, I live in peace and as far as I can, I purify my thoughts. What else can I do?' Then the old man stood up and stretched his hands towards heaven. His fingers became like ten lamps of fire and he said to him, 'If you will, you can become all flame.'[8]

Our potential and vocation is to be ignited by the Spirit, engulfed with his fire, radiant and ablaze with the Spirit himself, the divine flame. We need to allow ourselves to be scorched, singed, caressed by such a flame.

In what ways have you experienced the fire of the divine Spirit in your life? Has this been a comforting or disturbing experience?

Formed by water

Sedimentary rocks are formed at the earth's surface by the accumulation and cementation of fragments of earlier rocks, minerals and organisms. This process causes sediments or organic particles (detritus) to settle and accumulate within layers or strata. Laid down by the ebb and flow of ancient seas, these rocks develop layer upon layer, the fossils preserving memories of the ancient past: stubborn or enduring remnants or relics of bygone ages. Sandstones, shales and limestone are the most common examples.

Before being deposited, sediments are formed by weathering, or earlier rocks by erosion in a source area, and then transported to the place of deposition by water, wind, ice, mass movement or glaciers. Such rocks are laid down in water and shaped by the action of water: deposition, erosion, formation.

As we shall explore in Chapter 4, water has become an evocative symbol of the spiritual life. The Bible begins and closes with rivers of water, bespeaking creation and new creation. Christian baptism reminds us of the need to be flooded, engulfed, drenched and saturated by the waters of the Holy Spirit. Throughout our spiritual life we need the overflowing, inundating Spirit to irrigate the parched earth of our soul. Streams of grace need to percolate the soul.

St Teresa of Avila (1515–82) confesses: 'I cannot find anything more apt for the explanation of certain spiritual things than this element of water; for, as I am ignorant and my wit gives me no help and I am so fond of this element, I have looked at it more attentively than at other things.'[9] The question is: how will we allow the water of God's grace to touch our lives and reshape us? How can we develop our receptivity to such streams of grace?

> Let us suppose that we are looking at two fountains, the basins of which can be filled with water... These two large basins can be filled with water in different ways: the water in the one comes from a long distance, by means of numerous conduits and through human skill; but the other has been constructed at the very source of the water and fills without making any noise. If the flow of water is abundant, as in the case we are speaking of, a great stream still runs from it after it has been filled; no skill is necessary here, and no conduits have to be made, for the water is flowing all the time. The difference between this and the carrying of the water by means of conduits is, I think, as follows. The latter corresponds to the spiritual sweetness which, as I say, is produced by meditation. It reaches us by way of our thoughts; we meditate upon created things and fatigue the understanding; and when at last, by means of our own efforts, it comes, the satisfaction which it brings to the soul fills the basin, but in doing so makes a noise, as I have said.
>
> To the other fountain the water comes direct from its source, which is God, and, when it is his Majesty's will and he is pleased to grant us some supernatural favour, its coming is accompanied by the greatest peace and quietness and sweetness within ourselves.[10]

In this passage from *The Interior Castle*, written in 1577, Teresa suggests there are two ways of receiving the water of God. Either we can stand at a distance from the fountain of God and receive the water of the Spirit, as it were, mediated through man-made and lengthy aqueducts and conduits, miles of pipelines of active, often noisy, talkative prayer. This in fact creates a distance from the fountain. Or we can stand very close to the fountain of God, quieten our spirit, and change our prayer from an active thinking and striving style to a more receptive passive, drinking-in style. In what Teresa calls 'the Prayer of Quiet', we can drink directly and immediately of the river of the Spirit bubbling up in front of us. How close, she asks, are you to the fountain?

Celebrate the ebb and flow of your spiritual life over the years. In each movement of the tide there is erosion and deposition—a cutting down and a building up, little by little. Fragments of experience coalesce in the spiritual journey. Things get glued together so that tiny fragments, perhaps weaknesses by themselves, become a strength.

Transformed by upheaval and stress

Metamorphic rocks are formed by processes of transformation, gradual or sudden: where any rock type—sedimentary rock, igneous rock or another older metamorphic rock—has been subject to different temperature and pressure conditions than those in which the original rock was formed. This process is called metamorphism; meaning 'to change in form'. The result is a profound change in the physical properties and chemistry of the stone.

Deep beneath the ground there are unseen but powerful forces at work. Sediments buried deep underground are subject to heaving processes and enormous weights pushed upon them. As this happens they change in character. In addition, fault lines and tectonic processes such as continental collisions cause horizontal pressure, friction, distortion and reshaping. We can read the history of the earth by examining metamorphic rocks which have become exposed at the surface following erosion and uplift. Metamorphic rocks may have a painful history, but they produce the most stunning and beautiful rocks, including marble, quartzite and jade. Metamorphic rocks tell us that from our experience of compression, from our vulnerability, woundedness and brokenness, God can bring forth gems. The most precious creations come from those that are crushed.

What experiences does this evoke for you? Have you changed as a result of a rift or a collision of forces? What have been the most extreme forces at work in your life? What stresses have turned out to be creative and formative for you? Name the changes and shifts for yourself.

The rock of salvation

Today's pilgrim to Jerusalem can touch and encounter the very rock of Calvary, part of a complex in the Church of the Holy Sepulchre that makes up 'the rock of our salvation'. The Gospel accounts of the first Easter specifically mention rock. There is the tomb itself which Joseph of Arithamea had had cut into the rock cliff (*petra*). There is the mighty rock or *lithos* that attempted to seal the tomb of Christ and was blasted away in the resurrection events, according to Matthew. There is evidence that the rock of Calvary itself is part of an ancient quarry.

This rock is scarred and shattered. The rock of Calvary itself may have been left standing amid the ancient quarry outside the city wall precisely because it was useless; a deep fracture running from its top into the earth indicates that it was unsuitable for use in building—it became a rejected rock. In Matthew's Gospel, Sinai-like earthquakes attend both the crucifixion and resurrection: 'The earth shook, and the rocks were split' (Matthew 27:51; see also 28:2). The rock of Calvary is indeed battered and bruised to this day: its deep scar and fracture speak powerfully of the woundedness and vulnerability of Christ. To see this at the top of Calvary (by the Greek altar) or at the foot of Calvary (in the chapel of Adam) is to recall the pain, the bloodshed, of Christ himself. As Toplady sang: 'Rock of Ages, cleft for me, let me hide myself in thee.' This prompted St Francis, when receiving the stigmata on Mount Alverna, to pray in the cleft of rocks, because they reminded him of the gaping wounds of Christ. As the hymn *Anima Christi* puts it: 'Within thy wounds, hide me.'

Indeed, the first Christians, seeking to make sense of the event of Calvary, turned to the Hebrew scriptures and there they found texts which spoke of a rejected rock being used in God's rebuilding purposes for humanity: 'The stone that the builders rejected has become the chief cornerstone.' This verse from the Psalms (118:22) is used by different communities in the New Testament (quoted in Mark, Matthew and Luke in the Holy Week story, by Peter in his sermon in Acts 4:11 and by the writer of 1 Peter 2:7). Jesus is also understood as 'a stone one strikes against… a rock one stumbles over' (Isaiah 8:14–15). But such a stone becomes the keystone in the new work, the new temple God is building, for a further text from Isaiah inspired the first Christians: 'See, I am laying in Zion a foundation stone, a tested stone, a precious cornerstone, a sure foundation' (28:16). This is quoted in Romans (9:33) and 1 Peter (2:4–6). The wounded and fractured rock of Calvary, then, is at once a memorial to the crucifixion and a pointer to a new future. God uses rocks in his divine purposes!

Questions for reflection

1 Which of the three major rock types do you most identify with? Why?
2 Recalling forces in your life that may be constructive or destructive, what formative events or influences do you wish to celebrate?
3 What do you feel about any possible woundedness, vulnerabilities, cracks or fractures? Where are your strengths?

4 How would you describe the present texture of your soul? Does it feel vulnerable, flaky, malleable, crumbly? Are there sharp edges? Any brittle or fragile parts? Are there parts that feel cracked or scarred, weathered, hardened or flaky? Does your soul feel in any way gravelly or gritty? Is it veined or streaked by recurring themes? What is the colour of your soul?

5 What parts of you might be named as resistances to God's formative purposes? Are you experiencing any friction in relation to God? What can you do to be more responsive to the purposes of God—whether that is akin to his work of erosion and a wearing down, or of reshaping and building up?

Prayer exercise

Either

Draw a T-shaped line on a fresh page. Let the horizontal top line represent the surface that you present to the world—your lifestyle, your persona. Let the vertical line stand for your hidden life, your personal history, the story of your soul. Mark it off roughly into thirds: at the base, to represent your life aged 0–20; the middle section 20–50; the upper section (if appropriate) your life from 50 to the present. Create horizontal bands to represent the three main strata. Give them a name: what kind of rock were you at that stage? To left and right of this put bold arrows to express the key influences that shaped your spiritual life in these periods: demands put upon you, responsibilities, key relationships and any creative influences. Maybe there are also painful events like bereavement or difficult change that you need to note, too.

As you review this investigation of the levels and layers and composition of the 'geology of your soul', give thanks for God's presence and providence in your life. Express sorrow or penitence where you have perhaps been resistant to God's activity. But above all, celebrate with praise the way God has shaped and reshaped your life: the signs that you bear today that you have experienced the fire, the water, the transformation of the Holy Spirit! As you review the 'cross section' of your soul and discern the patterns and responses, use a prayer attributed to Macrina Wiederkehr: 'God, help me to believe the truth about myself, no matter how beautiful it may be.' Respond with both your head and your heart!

Importantly, conclude with drawing a massive and substantial rock mass at the base of your vertical line, underpinning all the strata: the immovable, unshakable, indestructible bedrock. Write on it: 'The Lord is my rock' or 'the rock was Christ' (1 Corinthians 10:4), or 'Christ my rock' or 'Christ, the core of my being'.

End with words from the seventh-century hymn:

> Christ is made the sure foundation, Christ the head and
>   cornerstone,
> chosen of the Lord, and precious, binding all the Church in one;
> holy Zion's help for ever, and her confidence alone.

Alternatively, conclude with the words of Psalm 18:2, 'The Lord is my rock, my fortress, and my deliverer, my God, my rock in whom I take refuge, my shield, and the horn of my salvation, my stronghold.'

Or

Take a stone and hold it in the palm of your hand. Take a close look at it and admire its uniqueness. Are there rough or smooth parts to it? There is only one just like this, with its particular markings and structure. Make friends with it! Its past: wonder to yourself—where has this stone come from? What is its past, its history? What great cliff or mountain was it once part of? What is its geological story? Wonder about what happened to this rock. Was it pounded by waves in the sea? Was it polished by the movement of ice? Its future: what will become of this stone? Will it be taken by a youth and thrown through a window? Or just lie unwanted on the ground? Will this stone be used by a craftsman in a structure: in a wall, in an art installation? Will it be carefully reshaped and remoulded by an artist or mason?

Finally, let this stone speak to you of your own life, past and future. You have a unique history and your own special gifting. Give thanks to God for his providence and provision. Thank God for your own 'markings'—those things about yourself, your appearance and personality that make you different. As you hold the stone in your hands, realise that God holds you lovingly in his hands. And he has plans for you. He desires to shape and reshape your life—to mould you into his image, to accomplish his work of formation in you, to use you in the great building work of his kingdom. Peter put it: 'like living stones, let yourselves be built into a spiritual house' (1 Peter 2:5). Rejoice that your life is raw material in the hands of the creator and redeemer God. Give thanks that he has an unfolding design and purpose for your unique life. Entrust yourself afresh to God, remembering: 'We are God's work of art' (Ephesians 2:10, JB).

2

Entering the cave of the heart: going deeper

'Teach me wisdom in my secret heart,' David prays (Psalm 51:6). In this chapter we begin to delve a little deeper and enter into the hidden chambers of our heart. We will be filled with awe and a sense of delight as we appreciate afresh our hidden spiritual beauty and our amazing capacity to experience the divine. We are ready to begin our descent.

Throughout the Holy Land mysterious and evocative caves of prayer summon the explorer and pilgrim. Near the oasis city of Jericho, clinging barnacle-like to the towering cliff face, the Monastery of the Temptation incorporates a remarkable cave where traditionally Jesus hid himself in his 40-day stay in the wilderness. It is certain that Jesus entered a cave to pray, as they are plentiful and inviting spaces of cool: caves are a characteristic feature of Judean monasticism to this day. Jesus enters his desert cave with these words ringing in his ears: 'You are my beloved Son; with you I am well-pleased.' This is the experience of enclosure: the embrace of God in the depths of the earth and in the depths of prayer. It is the place of intimacy with God. In the darkness of the cave Jesus allows himself to be held in the arms of his Father, taking deep within him the awesome affirmation made at his baptism. In his desert prayer, he is to explore the meaning of this.

The Desert Fathers and Mothers prayed in caves. Every monastic settlement in the Judean desert consisted of caves; a few are spacious, with a chapel area, and a sleeping and cooking area, but most are small, with just a ledge for a bed. The characteristic teaching of the Desert Fathers is summed up in the saying: 'Go, sit in your cell and your cell will teach you everything.'[1] Christ highlights the hiddenness of true prayer in the Sermon on the Mount, contrasting it with the false paraded prayer of street corners: 'When you pray, go to your private room, shut yourself in, and so pray to your Father… in that secret place' (Matthew 6:6, NJB). The word used for secret is *kruptos* denoting something hidden or concealed. We are being called to hiddenness where 'your life is hidden with Christ in God' (Colossians 3:3). In these desert caves one experiences a kind of deafening silence, the sort of silence that rings in your ears. There is a deep sense of being held by God, encompassed, enveloped, reassuring you. You are 'accepted in the Beloved' (Ephesians 1:6, NKJV).

At Bethlehem, located on the edge of the Judean desert, it is possible to wander through a network of caves adjoining the cave of the Nativity. Here Jerome in 386 makes a cave his place of prayer and study. With Paula, a widow, and some women ascetics, he organises the formation of an underground monastery. Bethlehem remains Jerome's home for the remaining 34 years of his life. Here he writes a large number of religious and literary works, but his greatest achievement is his translation of the Bible (the Old Testament from Hebrew, the New Testament from Greek) into the version which becomes the standard Latin text, the Vulgate.

In the Byzantine period, the Judean wilderness was flooded with monks seeking seclusion in caves. The title of Derwas Chitty's book sums up the phenomenon: *The Desert a City*. At the height of the Byzantine period in the sixth century AD, there were 70 monasteries in the Judean desert. Today one can visit caves of prayer in seven living monasteries. In the narrow ravine of the Wadi Faran, in the desert east of Jerusalem, we find the very first Judean monastery, founded in 275 by St Chariton. Today, a sole Russian monk occupies this cave complex, the silence broken only by the babble of the nearby spring and by birdsong echoing amid the sheer white cliffs. The Greek Orthodox monastic village of Mar Saba, dating from the fifth century and one of the oldest continually occupied monasteries in the world, has grown barnacle-like on the cliffs above the Kidron Valley. The 'God-built Church' is a massive cave consecrated for worship and prayer in 490. Also near Bethlehem are the fortress monasteries of St Theodosius and St Elias. In the depths of the Wadi Kelt a small community resides at St George of Kobiza, while clinging precariously to the precipitous cliffs above Jericho is, as we noted, the Monastery of the Temptation of Christ. Near the Jordan River, five miles north of the Dead Sea, lies the Greek Orthodox monastery of St Gerasimus. There are also ruins to be discovered: one can visit substantial remnants of the monastery of St Euthymius (377–473) who established the pattern for Palestinian monasticism by insisting that those who desired the eremitical (solitary) life were first trained in the cenobitic community. The remnants of one monastery are to be found in the scary Wadi Og. In his sixth-century account of the discovery of this site as a suitable place of prayer and retreat by Theoctistus and Euthymius, Cyril of Scythopolis gives us a vivid sense of the topography:

> As they passed through the desert they came to a terrifying gorge, extremely steep and impassable. On seeing the place and going round the cliffs above it they found, as if guided by God, a huge and marvellous cave in the northern cliff of the gorge. Not without danger they made the steep ascent and just managed to climb up to it. Overjoyed as if the cave had been prepared for them by God, they made it their home.[2]

St Anthony, considered the first ever monk, lived for years in the depths of a dark cave. The pilgrim may visit St Anthony's Cave hidden away on Mount Colzim, in a valley that runs down to the Red Sea in Egypt. It is high up in the cliff face, more than 2000 feet above sea level (he also utilised an underground cave, his water source). From the cliff face, you enter a dark, narrow tunnel, more than 20 feet in length, which finally reaches a chamber in pitch blackness. Inside there is a real sense of enclosure, of being held by God. It does not feel claustrophobic, but it does feel that you are in a deep mysterious place concealed from the world and from the blazing sunlight of the desert, wrapped around by the walls of living rock.

Such caves sometimes involve ascent, but often they invite us to leave behind the surface, the superficial, to descend and go deeper with God. What will the cave of your heart be like?

The call of the cave: Eastern perspectives

Basil of Caesarea (330–79) played a vital role in helping to bring the vision of desert monasticism to the wider world. He visited the monastic caves and settlements of Palestine, Syria and Egypt in order to discover their secret. On his return to Cappodocia he embodied his insights in his Rule which to this day remains central to Eastern monasticism, while Benedict acknowledges his debt to Basil in his own Rule which became the basis of Western monasticism. The stunning monastic caves at Goreme, decorated with astonishing frescoes, testify to the tradition that Basil began in Cappodocia. In his letter to his friend Gregory Nazianzus, written to persuade him to come and join his retreat, Basil explores four aspects of the call of the cave.[3]

First, the cave calls us to *stillness and silence*. Basil writes: 'One should aspire at keeping the mind in quietude [*hesychia*]...' The Desert Fathers echo this theme. The story is told:

> Abba Macarius the Great said to the brothers at Scetis, when he dismissed the assembly, 'Flee, my brothers.' One of the old men asked him, 'Where could we flee to beyond this desert?' He put his finger on his lips and said, 'Flee that,' and he went into his cell, shut the door and sat down.[4]

Second, the cave calls us to *solitude*. Basil explains: 'The solitude [*eremia*] offers a very great advantage for our task of prayer. Let us for a season be free from the commerce of men, so that nothing may come from without and break the continuity of the *ascesis* [training or discipline].' There is a place in discipleship for getting off the treadmill of work and activity, saying goodbye to the clamour of things in the world forever competing for our attention, in order that, for a while at least, we may become focused on God and utterly attentive to him.

Third, the cave calls us to *detachment*. Basil writes: 'Now this withdrawal [*anachoresis*, retreat] does not mean that we should leave the world bodily, but rather break loose from the ties of "sympathy" of the soul with the body.' Basil is extolling the virtues of making a retreat from activity, for a few minutes, or hours, or days. He says that, for a season, we have to cut our ties, loosen our grip and grasp on activities, let go of our attachments and of our worries. This is so we can become wholly available to God in prayer.

Fourth, the cave calls us to *receptivity*. The most important thing, says Basil, is that we are 'making ready to receive in our heart the imprint of divine teaching… beautiful is the prayer that impresses into the mind a clear notion of God.' For Basil and the Desert Fathers and Mothers, the overriding aim is to learn to listen out for the whisper of God's voice and to discern his will and guidance.

Castle underground: Western perspectives

Teresa of Avila (1515–82) employs vivid images to describe the changes that can take place in prayer. In *The Interior Castle*, depicting the soul as a crystal castle with many rooms, with Christ dwelling at the centre, she invites the reader to trace a journey through successive stages in order to reach a state of mystical union. We might take the liberty to read this through the lens of underground spirituality: the rooms become caves! The castle relocates underground, and we can read the rooms as subterranean chambers on different levels which we stumble into as explorers of the interior spaces of the heart:

I began to think of the soul as if it were a castle made of a single diamond or of very clear crystal, in which there are many rooms, just as in Heaven there are many mansions. Now if we think carefully over this, the soul of the righteous one is nothing but a paradise, in which, as God tells us, He takes His delight. For what do you think a room will be like which is the delight of a King so mighty, so wise, so pure and so full of all that is good? I can find nothing with which to compare the great beauty of a soul and its great capacity… (though) the very fact that His majesty says it is made in His image means that we can hardly form any conception of the soul's great dignity and beauty…

Let us imagine that this castle contains many mansions, some above, others below, others at each side; and in the centre and midst of them all is the chiefest mansion where the most secret things pass between God and the soul.[5]

The image conveys the beauty and potential of the soul; the door to the castle, and indeed its weaving corridor, is the experience of prayer. Rowan Williams observes:

If the soul is a home for God, it is a home with an enormous abundance of rooms, and we shall need to know where we are if we are not to be deceived and think we have encountered God when we have not… the journey inward is a journey to the place where God's love meets and mingles with the life of the soul, and thus we need to keep moving through the rooms until we find the middle of what sounds remarkably like a maze… We do not know where the boundaries are if we never move forward and walk into them… We need to know what we are capable of, positively and negatively.[6]

The first three 'caves' represent an increasing detachment from the things of the world and a process of deepening repentance and humility. In the first room of self-knowledge, we start to realise that we are made for God. In the second cave we are called to conquer the pull to turn back to the attractions of the world, in order to remain very focused and single-minded on the interior journey. The third cave represents the stability and predictability of respectable routines and normal disciplines of the Christian life, like active discursive meditation. A sign or indicator that the soul is ready to move on from these reveals itself in a holy restlessness or discontent with unfulfilling dutiful praying—a craving for a greater interior freedom and a desire to jump off the treadmill of Christian life.

A significant turning point in the journey comes with entry into the voluminous and spacious fourth cave, a place of new discovery which opens us up to 'supernatural prayer': 'Supernatural prayer is where God takes over. It is also called infused contemplation, passive prayer, mystical prayer, or infused prayer. All labels, again, mean the same thing. This type of prayer means that God is communicating with the person.'[7] Teresa advises: 'the important thing is not to think much, but to love much.'[8] A letting go of former restrictive practices of prayer enables a movement from the primacy of ego to the initiative of God.

But there is no need to rest even here: we can go deeper into God if we have the courage to keep moving. The fifth cave is a place of liberation where the soul breaks free from its chrysalis or cocoon and learns to 'fly' in a new freedom. In the sixth, the pilgrim soul stumbles on a glittering treasury concealed in the inner depths: a storehouse of spiritual gifts. Here Teresa speaks of the soul's betrothal to God, while in the seventh she uses the daring language of mystical marriage to describe union with God as an abiding awareness and permanent consciousness of unity with the indwelling Christ. As Teresa provides a sketch of the spiritual life through the imagery of one room or cave leading to another in a mysterious castle of prayer, the main point is this: whatever cave of prayer you find yourself in, this cave has an enticing tunnel opposite the way in, beckoning you to yet-unexplored reaches of prayer. Don't get stuck in one cave. Go on, attempt the next passageway, see where it leads!

Four challenges for cavers

1. Unblock the entrance

Sometimes caves can become forgotten because they are overgrown by foliage. Other caves have entrances that have become constricted because of the accumulation of rubbish or debris, silt, rocks and earth washed down the hillside in times of storm. The prerequisite for the Christian explorer is first of all to rediscover the entry point to the cave of the heart, to make contact with the bare rock floor. It is a question of gaining access to one's own depths. We need to identify anything that is blocking the entrance to prayer—undue attachments, the clutter of life's activities. It is a hard task to remove and let go of these, but if they have become a barrier or impediment to prayer we must be decisive. There is the task of clearing up to do. John the Baptist called people to unblock and open up a way for God by facing up to their sins through confession and repentance, quoting Isaiah 40: 'In the wilderness prepare the way of the Lord, make straight in the desert a highway for our God. Every valley shall be lifted up, and every mountain and hill be made low; the uneven ground shall become level, and the rough places a plain. Then the glory of the Lord shall be revealed...' (Isaiah 40:3–5).

2 Celebrate the beauty of the cave

Celebrate the mystery and wonder of your own being. The metaphor of the cave is linked closely with the biblical symbol of the heart.[9] The *Catechism of the Catholic Church* reminds us that

> according to Scripture, it is the heart that prays... The heart is the dwelling-place where I am, where I live; according to the Semitic or biblical expression, the heart is the place 'to which I withdraw'. The heart is our hidden centre... the place of encounter, because as image of God we live in relation.[10]

Moreover, according to the Hebraic tradition, the heart is the centre of the human, uniting the intellectual, emotional and volitional functions of the person.[11] It stands as a potent symbol of the inner life that is embodied and incarnate. As Ware reminds us, in Orthodox theology

> the heart signifies the deep self; it is the seat of wisdom and understanding, the place where our moral decisions are made, the inner shrine in which we experience divine grace and the indwelling of the Holy Trinity. It indicates the human person as a 'spiritual subject,' created in God's image and likeness.[12]

Rejoice in your potentiality! Richard Rohr tells us: 'The most courageous thing we will ever do is to bear humbly the mystery of our own reality.'[13]

3 Descend with the mind in the heart

Eastern perspectives celebrate the potentialities of prayer within the human person. The divinely formed faculty that apprehends God is called the *nous*, the spiritual mind or intuitive intellect. It is carefully distinguished from *dianoia*, the faculty of reason: 'The intellect does not function by formulating abstract concepts... it understands divine truth by means of immediate experience, intuition or "simple cognition"... It is the organ of contemplation.'[14] Ware puts it: 'Here is no head-heart dichotomy, for the intellect is within the heart. The heart is the meeting point between body and soul, between the subconscious, conscious and supraconscious, between the human and the divine.'[15]

Symeon the New Theologian (949–1022), whom we will meet again in Chapter 4, writes of *moving* or relocating the mind to the heart: 'The mind should be in the heart... Keep your mind there (in the heart), trying by every possible means to find the place where the heart is, in order that, having found it, your mind should constantly abide there. Wrestling thus, your mind will find the place of the heart.'[16]

Indeed, we are invited to a participation in God. Fourteenth-century Gregory Palamas of Mount Athos, a main proponent of the prayer of *hesychia* (stillness), puts it: 'In prayer… man is called to participation in divine life: this participation is also the true knowledge of God.'[17] In his controversy with the Calabrian philosopher Barlaam, Palamas is insistent: 'But hesychasts know that the purified and illuminated mind, when clearly participating in the grace of God, also beholds other mystical and supernatural visions…'[18] Palamas represents developments from the seminal thinking of Evagrius of Pontus (346–99) who very succinctly expressed the intermingling waters of spirituality and theology: 'He who prays is a theologian; a theologian is one who prays.'[19] As Russian mystic Theophan the Recluse puts it, prayer 'descends with the mind into the heart'. Seraphim of Sarov advises us to 'guard the heart'.

4 Abide

If we have decisively taken steps downwards into the soul, and have determinedly let go, for the moment, of surface cares, what happens now? If we have taken our thinking or pondering mind with us into the cave of the heart, what comes next? What goes on in the cave?

> Abide in me as I abide in you… Those who abide in me and I in them bear much fruit, because apart from me you can do nothing… As the Father has loved me, so I have loved you; abide in my love. If you keep my commandments, you will abide in my love, just as I have kept my Father's commandments and abide in his love. I have said these things to you so that my joy may be in you, and that your joy may be complete.
> JOHN 15:4–5, 9–11

The Greek word *meno* which we translate as 'abide' has a rich range of meanings. It can be translated by these words—which become imperatives from the mouth of Christ: stay, wait, linger, remain, stand your ground. Or we might say, when you find yourself in the cave of the heart, stay at it, don't wriggle—allow yourself to be held by God in the stillness. See what happens next! (We will be exploring this in later chapters.) But, for the present, in this hyperactive and frantic world, just abide. Prayer is the portal of the soul. Enjoy a sense of the abode—for this is in some sense a homecoming. Richard Foster calls prayer 'finding the heart's true home'. He writes:

> For too long we have been in a far country: a country of noise and hurry and crowds, a country of climb and push and shove, a country of frustration and fear and intimidation. God welcomes us home: home to serenity and peace and joy, home to friendship and fellowship and openness, home to intimacy and acceptance and affirmation.[20]

This, ultimately, is the invitation of prayer in the cave of the heart. In his canticle 'The Living Flame of Love' John of the Cross celebrates our great capacity and potentiality for welcoming God in our lives:

> *O lamps of fire*
> *in whose splendours*
> *the deep caverns of feeling,*
> *once obscure and blind,*
> *now give forth, so rarely, so exquisitely,*
> *both warmth and light to their Beloved.*

He explains:

> These caverns are the soul's faculties: memory, intellect and will. They are deep as the boundless goods of which they are capable since anything less than the infinite fails to fill them… when these caverns are empty and pure, the thirst, hunger, and yearning of the spiritual feeling is intolerable…

Go on, says St John, keep the caverns of the soul as uncluttered as possible, and as expectant as possible, for the mysterious advent of God into our depths. Thirst and long for the wisdom, the love and the very presence of God![21]

Questions for reflection

1 How would you describe the entry of the 'cave of your heart'? Is its entrance open or cluttered? Do you notice any stumbling blocks which impede access—to God, to others? Can you name any self-protective barriers—aspects of your personal armoury—that fence others from entry?

2 How would you describe the state of the 'cave of your heart'? Is your heart's cave voluminous, with a great capacity for God, a spaciousness of soul? Or do you find it is in some way narrow or constricted? Is it a receptive, hospitable, welcoming space or wary, tight, cautious? Do you need to take chisel in hand and expand your heart, carving out more space for God? Pray with the psalmist: 'You shall enlarge my heart' (Psalm 119:32, NKJV).

3 How would you describe the ecology of your soul? What contributes to the climate, the environment, of the cave of the heart? What is keeping it healthy and life-giving, a place of growth? Is anything threatening your spiritual growth or becoming a barrier to it?

4 Tracing your way with the help of Teresa's map, what kind of cave of prayer do you find yourself in right now? Which is the next one that beckons?

5 Which of Basil's recommendations speaks most forcefully to you? Why?

Prayer exercise

Either

This is a way of practising a prayer that is first introvert in character, then extrovert. First, close your arms around your chest: let this speak to you of the experience of enclosure, being held by God. Feel enfolded and hemmed in by God's unconditional love. Permit yourself to be overwhelmed by God. Rest in this experience, as Jesus rested in the cave. As the Desert Fathers put it: 'Sit in your cell, and your cell will teach you everything.'

Then begin to open your arms wide. Let this bespeak utter exposure to God: open yourself to the wind of God's Spirit. Stay in this mode as long as you can. What does it feel like? What is God saying to you?

After the prayer exercise, ask yourself: how did that feel? Take stock of your responses and reactions. What is holding you back from utter exposure to God? Name your barriers, fears, hesitations. What is your experience of being held by God? What feelings or effects on you did it produce?

Or

In the Orthodox tradition the phrase 'prayer of the heart' denotes the Jesus Prayer: 'Lord Jesus Christ, Son of God, have mercy on me a sinner.' Practise this now. Breathe in deeply on the first phrase, inhaling the name of Jesus, and breathe out on the second phrase, exhaling and expelling any attitudes as a 'sinner'. Sometimes people note three stages of progress in the practice of the Jesus Prayer. First comes verbal prayer, as you repeat the words out loud, moving your lips. A second stage is denoted mental prayer: the Prayer becomes silent or mental and is repeated not outwardly but in the mind. Finally, the Jesus Prayer becomes a continuous prayer in the heart, united as it were with the rhythms of your own heartbeat. It has descended to the very centre of your being, the cave of the heart.[22]

3

Plunging beneath the waters: the hidden river of prayer

From deep below us we can hear the intriguing sound of water gushing forth. Listen for a moment to its musical murmur. It is splashing and gurgling in the depths of our being—sometimes roaring in full flood, sometimes babbling or trickling as a gentle subterranean stream. In this chapter we will dip into the river of prayer and find it to be mysterious and life-giving. We will encounter God as a river of divine life engulfing us, energising us, inundating us, reinvigorating us. We will learn to swim underground!

Beneath the ancient city of Jerusalem flows a secret, life-giving river. Indeed, together with the mysterious Rock, the sacred space later to be called Mount Moriah or Mount Zion, it is the very key to the existence of the holy city, first for the Canaanites and later for the Israelites. 'There is a river whose streams make glad the city of God' (Psalm 46:4). The secret river emerges as the spring of Gihon—which means 'gushing': it pours out a vast quantity of water for 30 minutes and then the flow subsides for hours. Solomon channelled the waters to irrigate his garden (2 Kings 25:4), but when it was feared that invading Assyrians might thieve or poison the supply (2 Chronicles 32:30) it was decided to camouflage the emerging brook and redirect the flow so that it emerged inside, not outside the city walls of the time. Hezekiah oversaw the excavation of a tunnel through the solid rock, the diggers beginning at opposite ends. They left an inscription to celebrate their meeting deep underground:

> Behold the tunnel. This is the story of its cutting. While the miners swung their picks, one towards the other, and when there remained only 3 cubits to cut, the voice of one calling his fellow was heard—for there was a resonance in the rock coming from both north and south. So the day they broke through the miners struck, one against the other, pick against pick, and the water flowed from the spring towards the pool, 1200 cubits. The height of the rock above the head of the miners was 100 cubits.[1]

The tunnels of the excavators meet just 10 cm off centre, a great engineering feat for the sixth century BC! Today's pilgrim may wade through the waters of Hezekiah's tunnel, taking a torch to dispel the pitch darkness. The passage is narrow and low in parts, and the water is generally knee level. One begins at the excavations of the City of David, and passes the entry to Warren's Shaft, the vertical cutting first exploited by the Jebusites in a fissure in the rock, which enabled water to be hauled up to the settlement. The pilgrim emerges at the Pool of Siloam, where Jesus told the blind man to wash his eyes (John 9) and from where water was drawn for the great annual event of the Feast of Tabernacles. Chapter 7 of John's Gospel gives us the dramatic cry of Christ:

> On the last day of the festival, the great day, while Jesus was standing there, he cried out, 'Let anyone who is thirsty come to me, and let the one who believes in me drink. As the scripture has said, "Out of the believer's heart shall flow rivers of living water."' Now he said this about the Spirit, which believers in him were to receive, for as yet there was no Spirit, because Jesus was not yet glorified.
>
> JOHN 7:37–39

The great Jewish festival of Tabernacles, with its vision of the river of God, forms the context of these words. Jesus attends the temple liturgy where Ezekiel's vision (ch. 47) was proclaimed to the pilgrims: a spring of God's generous blessing will one day burst forth from under the altar of the temple and spill out to bring renewal to the whole world. In the ceremony, water in golden pitchers was carried up the steep hill of Zion, from the Pool of Siloam, to the temple on the crest of the Ophel Ridge, and poured out as a visual sign of this vision.

North of the temple area is sited the Pool of Bethesda. Here mineral-rich springs bubbling up from deep below the city were first exploited by the Romans as the site became an *asclepium*, or healing centre. Jesus encounters a paralytic there 'waiting for the stirring of the water; for an angel of the Lord went down at certain seasons into the pool, and stirred up the water; whoever stepped in first after the stirring of the water was made well from whatever disease that person had' (John 5:3–4). Jesus becomes the healing stream himself as he leads the patient to wholeness.

An underground river of prayer

The imagery of a river expresses for us key aspects of prayer. Like a hidden spring or underground river, prayer is often unseen, unrecognised, elusive but having powerful influences. Prayer as a secret river remains something that cannot be measured or quantified. It is something essentially mysterious, but rises to the surface and reveals its presence in a number of different expressions. Roose-Evans puts it:

> This secret life with God is like an underground river... we cannot see it, but we know it is there. Like water diviners we sense its presence within ourselves and also in others. We know it is there, even though others may doubt and challenge its reality. God is an underground river flowing to the sea... The underground river flows through each one of us.[2]

The image of water in the scriptures is predominantly concerned not with cleansing but with giving life, often associated with the work of the Holy Spirit. In John's Gospel we are led to Jacob's Well, symbol of humanity's thirst—it is deep, and taps into the underground reserves of Samaria. Jesus says: 'If you knew the gift of God… you would have asked him, and he would have given you living water… those who drink of the water that I will give them will never be thirsty. The water that I will give will become in them a spring of water gushing up to eternal life' (4:10, 14). Jesus promises a Spirit who quenches our deepest thirst, an inner geyser, welling up to eternal life. The woman represents all of humanity in her cry: 'Sir, give me this water' (John 4:15). A twelfth-century Armenian poet puts it:

> O Fountain of life, you asked for water from the woman of
>   Samaria,
> And promised her living water, in return for the transitory one.
> Grant to me, O Fountain of Life,
> That holy drink for my soul,
> That flows from the heart in rivers,
> The Spirit from whom grace gushes forth.[3]

'God is an underground river,' Meister Eckhart said, 'that no one can dam up or stop.'[4] David Anderson writes:

> I love that image of God because it completely flips the dominant image of God 'up there.' When we first imagine a deity, God is always 'up,' always distant, the Sky God of nearly every ancient religion. Until gradually it dawns upon us that the God whom the cosmos cannot contain is actually deep within. The ground of our being. And that underground river runs right through you. Sink a well within yourself and in the hidden darkness of your soul the river erupts. Water! Through the prophet God promises even 'streams in the desert'. God is the subterranean gusher and prayer is the well. Draw deeply— and often.[5]

The hidden river is a symbol of divine creativity and re-creation: 'a stream would rise from the earth, and water the whole face of the ground—then the Lord God formed man… A river flows out of Eden to water the garden' (Genesis 2:6–7, 10; cf. 1:1). In the Apocalypse 'the Lamb… will guide them to springs of the water of life' (Revelation 7:17). The vision concludes:

> Then the angel showed me the river of the water of life, bright as crystal, flowing from the throne of God and of the Lamb through the middle of the street of the city. On either side of the river is the tree of life… producing its fruit each month; and the leaves of the tree are for the healing of the nations.
> REVELATION 22:1–2

So the river is at once a primordial and eschatological image of the divine life, bubbling at the beginning and the end.

The river is also an image which reflects diversity and flexibility. As rivers have different characteristics as they flow through the terrain, from incisive fast-flowing torrents to meandering ponderous currents, so prayer goes through various phases and embraces different intensities. The diversity of prayer encompasses turbulence and confusion as well as contemplative peace. The river is only part of the ecosystem. It has a significant part to play in the shaping of the landscape but remains one factor among many. Prayer too fulfils important functions within the ecosystem of Christian formation but is not the whole story, pointing to a diversity of human factors and resistances that come into play. As an underground river will course through different geologies (the great biblical river of the Jordan itself flowing along a fault line), so prayer will encounter both resistance and weakness.

Dark waters

John of the Cross speaks about 'dark waters'. When he was incarcerated in the dark cave of Toledo's prison, the only sound he could hear was the trickle of the river deep below him. Through repentance we prepare ourselves to experience the inflow of God's dark waters into the soul. John writes of 'the fortitude this obscure, painful, and dark water of God bestows on the soul… after all, even though it is dark, it is water, and thereby refreshes and fortifies the soul in what most suits it—although in darkness, and painfully.'[6] For John, the waters can denote the experience of prayer or the experience of God. The waters flow together imperceptibly. In his poem 'The Fountain' John celebrates this night-time flow:

> For I know well the spring that flows and runs,
> although it is night
> I know well the stream that flows from this spring is mighty in
>   compass and power,
> although it is night.[7]

Sometimes prayer is experienced as a turbulent place, with eddies, whirlpools, rapids and unexpectedly strong currents. Prayer is now a torrent where boulders, other detritus and rubbish get forced along. The river of prayer becomes a place of attrition and erosion, where stones get their corners knocked off. But prayer can also at the same time be experienced as a place of profound transformation and creativity, where a new identity is being shaped and formed. Waters can break down and build up. The story of Jacob's wrestling with God in the swirling waters of the Jabbok (Genesis 32:22–32) has become symbolic of the struggle of prayer. From the outset, as von Rad notes, the story was archetypal and representative: 'It contains experiences of faith that extend from the most ancient period down to the time of the narrator… as it is now related it is clearly transparent as a type of that which Israel experienced from time to time with God.'[8] It is the struggle of humanity with God. Jacob wrestled and fought with a Stranger, an unknown figure; he later described this encounter by saying, 'I have seen God face to face.' It was indeed a case of divine–human combat.[9]

Amid the swirling currents, Jacob experiences a barrier or frontier becoming a threshold or place of transition.[10] Seen as an encounter with God, this story casts light on the experience of prayer because it is precisely in the waters of struggle, in the darkness and in the experience of being wounded by God, that Jacob receives his new name and new identity: no longer is he 'Grasper' (Jacob) but 'One who struggles with God' (Israel). This profound affirmation comes in the midst of solitude: 'Jacob was left alone' (Genesis 32:24). For Jacob this meant a letting go, for the moment, of attachments to people and possessions. He was prepared to part from family and to stand alone before God. Prayer becomes a place of honesty and naked exposure to God, a place of risk and vulnerability where God is allowed both to wound and to bless.

Jacob is brought to a point of brokenness. His running symbolised his independence, his desire to escape uncomfortable truths and conflicts, his evasion of God and his determination to stay in control of his life. Now Jacob can run no longer: he can only limp, for God touches him and disables him. He is reduced to a state of new dependency on God himself. This wounding of Jacob represents God finally melting his wilfulness and paralysing his defiant ego. For the moment, at least, he crumples up: God has the mastery. In giving Jacob a new identity God affirms the role of struggling in an evolving relationship with him. It is not to be avoided but faced: those who embrace their struggles with God can emerge with a clearer sense of identity and mission. Jacob's experience in the dark waters actually equips him to face the next stage of his journey. The torrent of prayer can be experienced as a place of profound growth, as we become wounded healers—as Nouwen says: 'For a deep understanding of our own pain makes it possible for us to convert our weakness into strength and to offer our own experience as source of healing.'[11] Brueggemann puts it, noting the significance of Jacob's struggle for Christians: 'This narrative reflects some of Israel's most sophisticated theology... God is God... Jacob is a cripple with a blessing... This same theology of weakness in power and power in weakness turns this text towards the New Testament and the gospel of the cross.'[12]

Knowing, being, doing: three dimensions of the underground river of prayer

1 A river of wisdom: the transformation of knowing

'"Out of the believer's heart shall flow rivers of living water." Now he said this about the Spirit, which believers in him were to receive' (John 7:38–39). Paul too alludes to such a river or current: 'God's love has been poured [*ekkechutai*, literally, "streamed forth profusely"] into our hearts through the Holy Spirit that has been given to us' (Romans 5:5). Both St John and St Paul point us towards the role of the Spirit in our discovery of God.

In John's Gospel, the Holy Spirit is understood as the teacher of disciples: 'The Advocate, the Holy Spirit… will teach you everything' (John 14:26). Lincoln puts it: 'part of his work as Advocate for the disciples in their mission to the world is to give them the requisite insight into Jesus' teaching… unfolding [its] significance for the new situation in which the disciples find themselves.'[13]

John develops this further: 'When the Spirit of truth comes, he will guide you into all the truth… he will take what is mine and declare it to you' (John 16:13, 14). The Spirit 'both reiterates what Jesus has said (cf. 14:26) and says more (16:13). What more he says is all the truth and all God's truth (v.15).'[14] Brodie observes here 'an advancing process of revelation'.[15] William Temple writes: 'The disciple is not to clamour for the solution of perplexities or for intellectual mastery of divine mysteries. What knowledge he has in this realm is his because the Spirit has declared it to him; and for the Spirit's declaration he must wait.'[16]

In Paul's thought the Holy Spirit effects a revelatory role, exposing us to deep wisdom:

> We speak God's wisdom, secret and hidden, which God decreed before the ages for our glory… as it is written, 'What no eye

has seen, nor ear heard, nor the human heart conceived, what God has prepared for those who love him'—these things God has revealed to us through the Spirit; for the Spirit searches everything, even the depths of God.

1 CORINTHIANS 2:7, 9–10

For Paul, the Holy Spirit works at a very deep level: 'The Spirit thus enables inward apprehension of profound divine truth.'[17] Kinn observes: 'Paul's point is that the Spirit alone is capable of revealing the mystery of God, since only the Spirit has intimate knowledge of God.'[18] Paul contrasts divine *Sophia*, manifest in Christ crucified (1 Corinthians 2:2), with worldly wisdom that cannot grasp God's upside-down ways. He advocates a particular way of approaching the study of divine things. He is insistent on the task of 'interpreting spiritual things to those who are spiritual' (1 Corinthians 2:13).

Christians must be *didaktois pneumatos*, 'taught by the Spirit', for divine truths are 'discerned spiritually'—'investigated spiritually' in Barrett's translation (1 Corinthians 2:14). Paul here gives us the basis for a Christian pattern of learning that is explicitly and self-consciously alerted to the role of the Spirit. He concludes with the claim 'We have the mind of Christ' (1 Corinthians 2:16).

The Spirit's gifting of wisdom has been celebrated throughout the history of Christian spirituality in the dynamic language of a river. Andrew of Crete exults in words sung today in Compline in the Orthodox Church: 'the Rock with the cleft from which the river of wisdom like a chalice pours forth streams of theology'. Hildegard of Bingen cries out: 'The soul that is full of wisdom is saturated with the spray of a bubbling fountain—God himself.'[19]

The quest for wisdom has been a theme that has occupied recent writers.[20] David Ford calls attention in this information age to our sense of being overwhelmed by an excess of information and data. The challenge is to dare to swim in the river or ocean of wisdom:

... we have to swim in wisdom. If we try to stay in control through information, knowledge and skills, keeping our feet safely on the bottom of the ocean, we drown. So we see an educational system drowning in information, knowledge and skills and rarely even attending to the question: how can we learn and teach wisdom?[21]

2 A fountain of holiness: the transformation of being

A second dimension in which the waters of the Spirit bring transformation is the area of 'being'. This invites us to a certain growth in self-awareness, spiritual development and understanding of vocation.

The Pauline writings employ the language of continuous transformation into Christ: 'Though our outer nature is wasting away, our inner nature is being renewed every day' (2 Corinthians 4:16, RSV). We welcome transcendence into our lives: 'we have this treasure in earthen vessels, to show that the transcendent power belongs to God and not to us' (2 Corinthians 4:7, RSV). Paul teaches that the Christian's calling and vocation, indeed destiny, is 'to be conformed to the image of his Son' (Romans 8:29). Ziesler puts it: 'Bearing his image is being like him, and representing him.'[23] The Greek idea *summorphosis* means 'to be formed or fashioned like, to be shaped like'. Inner lives are to be reshaped according to the pattern of Christ; personal resources and aptitudes to be realigned to the template of Christ. This is growth in Christlikeness: 'My little children, with whom I am again in travail until Christ be formed (*morphothe*) in you!' (Galatians 4:19, RSV). John develops this in terms of *homoiosis* or assimilation to God (1 John 3:2). We are called to be ever more alert to what has traditionally been termed 'sanctification' or growth in holiness: a veritable and verifiable growth in virtue and character.

3 A stream of energy: the transformation of doing

A third dimension of the Spirit's work in us is revealed by Luke. The Spirit of God energises and makes possible the liberating ministry of Jesus (Luke 4). In Luke, the Holy Spirit comes to Jesus when he is at prayer (Luke 3:21–22) and Jesus teaches his disciples to pray for the Holy Spirit whom the Father longs to give in response to our searching (Luke 11:13). The risen Christ promises the apostles: 'You will receive power [*dunamis*] when the Holy Spirit has come upon you; and you will be my witnesses' (Acts 1:8). Stronstad says: 'In this dominical saying Luke gives his readers the key to interpreting the purpose of the gift of the Spirit, not only to the disciples on the day of Pentecost but also throughout Luke-Acts… the gift of the Spirit always results in mission.'[24]

Theologians freely use metaphor to describe the empowering of the Spirit. Moltmann is inspired by Meister Eckhart's depiction of the Spirit of God as a great underground river which rises to the surface in springs and fountainheads:

> Out of God, blessing and the energies of life spill over onto the whole of creation (Psalm 65:9); from this fountain people receive 'grace upon grace' (John 1:16). Jesus talks about… 'a spring of water welling up eternal life' (John 4:14). The 'well of life' is not in the next world, and not in the church's font: it is in human beings themselves. If they receive the life-giving water, they themselves become the wellspring of this water for other people.[25]

Moltmann commends what he calls 'mystical metaphors' to explore the experience of the Spirit: 'In the mystical metaphors, the distance between a transcendent subject and its immanent work is ended… the divine and human are joined in an organic cohesion.'[26] Gutiérrez says: 'spirituality is indeed like living water that springs up in the very depths of the experience of faith.'[27] The streams of the Spirit flow imperceptibly within the river of prayer. Such life-giving waters are the key to Christian formation.

The waters of baptism

John Taylor, in his seminal book on the Holy Spirit, also points us towards the life-giving waters of the Spirit:

Baptism has so often been treated simply as a rite de passage which, having been passed through, is left behind, that the church has largely forgotten to see in its waters the symbol of that element in which the Christian lives and moves and has his being, namely the Spirit himself. He does not leave those waters behind but lives on in their meaning.

He goes on:

We must allow the awesome archetypal resonances of the water symbol to fill out our understanding of our baptism and of that life in the Spirit which it represents... The Holy Spirit is totally primordial. His is the elemental force beyond all other forces... the force of love.[28]

This river of the Spirit energises and animates Christian formation and ministry. Do not stay stranded on the bank: dare to enter the risky waters! Baptism is not a one-off event in the lives of Christians. Rather it sets the pattern for the whole of the Christian life. We pass through the baptismal waters at the beginning, but we are called to be a pilgrim people through all of life. Each Easter Christians revisit their baptism and remind themselves that they are called from death to life. As the baptismal liturgy puts it:

Through the deep waters of death you brought your Son, and raised him to life in triumph... We thank you, Father, for the water of Baptism: in it we are buried with Christ in his death. By it we share in his resurrection. Through it we are reborn by the Holy Spirit.[29]

But all through the year God is calling us to step into the swirling waters, to wade into the deep, to drown our small ideas, let go of certain dreams or sins, to submerge our narrowed hopes or worn-out practices and to hear again the call of Christ. We are a baptismal people, a river people, who allow the waters of prayer to course through our life. God is always calling us to go deeper. John Henry Newman put it:

> For in truth we are not called once only, but many times; all through our life Christ is calling us. He called us first in Baptism; but afterwards also; whether we obey his voice or not, He graciously calls us still… He calls us on from grace to grace, and from holiness to holiness, while life is given us… we are all in the course of calling, on and on, from one thing to another…[30]

Questions for reflection

1 How do find yourself responding to the idea of prayer as a hidden river flowing through your life? How does this resonate with your experience? What metaphor or image would you choose to describe the role of prayer in your life?
2 What do you thirst for most?
3 Meister Eckhart described the Spirit of God as a great underground river which rises to the surface in springs. What is the evidence, outer or inner, in your life that indicates the hidden, secret presence of the Spirit deep within?
4 How is the river of prayer flowing in your life right now? Is it a turbulent river, with eddies and whirlpools, or calm and gently flowing? Do you identify with Jacob's experience (Genesis 32) in any way?

Prayer exercise

The leader slowly pours water into a large bowl as a visual focus and reminder of baptism.

In his glorious promise of the river of God Jesus suggests three steps his disciples need to take: 'Let anyone who is thirsty come to me, and let the one who believes in me drink. As the scripture has said, "Out of the believer's heart shall flow rivers of living water"' (John 7:37–38). In our prayer we can take these three steps: we thirst, come to Jesus and drink afresh of the Spirit of God.

First acknowledge and recognise your thirst for the Spirit: spend some moments yearning and longing for more of the water of the Spirit in your life. Hold in your imagination the scene of an arid landscape, a thirsty desert representing your soul. Imagine that there are springs and water-courses below you in the ground.

Second, come to Jesus, the giver of the Spirit, and place yourself in expectant relation to him. Picture Jesus standing by a gushing fountain, springing up from the ground, pointing to it invitingly.

Third, we are invited to drink and receive afresh the living water. Imbibe the living waters. Drink in the Spirit. Ask the Holy Spirit to quench and fulfil your deepest thirst.

4

Carving out cisterns:
resources and reserves

Where do you turn to when you run dry? What reserves can you draw on when your soul is parched and arid? What resources can you fall back on when you can't pray? What waters of spirituality and wisdom can you tap when you need to quench the deep thirst in your soul? It is time for us to sink boreholes, to open up wells and to carve out cisterns. It is time for us to discover underground springs that will refresh and replenish the soul. They are always there, but we need to map them, to note them, so we can access them when needed.

The pilgrim to the Holy Land encounters the issue of water at every turn. An itinerary in the Holy Land will include many encounters with wells: Mary's well at Nazareth, the well of the vineyard at Ein Karem, and Jacob's Well at Shechem (present-day Nablus).

Pilgrims are exhorted, especially in the summer months, always to carry water—dehydration can be a real problem. Pilgrims will visit archaeological sites, such as Masada and Caesarea Maritima, that include astonishing cisterns and aqueducts. From 'Dan to Beer Sheba', the ancient designation for the Holy Land (see for example 1 Kings 4:25), the most pressing issue has always been the supply of water. At Dan, the meltwaters of the mighty snow-capped Mount Hermon flow out to become the headwaters of the Jordan, while at Beer Sheba in the south, we can still see Abraham's ancient well (see Genesis 21:25–34; 26:14–33). Beneath the ancient archaeological tell an extraordinary complex of cisterns and channels were excavated in the ninth century BC to garner the precious water; they are vast,

Leabharlanna Poibli Chathair Bhaile Átha Cliath
Dublin City Public Libraries

cavernous spaces, with a capacity of holding 184,000 gallons: hewn out of the living rock, their walls are plastered over to prevent seepage.

Jerusalem itself was established where it was precisely because of water, as we noted; the very designation 'Zion' may derive etymologically from 'thirsty place' or 'arid place'—significant physically and spiritually. Today the pilgrim can enter the vast 'cistern of St Helena' beneath the Coptic property near the Church of the Resurrection (the Holy Sepulchre) and is invited to sing hymns that will resound and echo around the great cavernous space, to the accompaniment of dripping water! One sees the Islamic *sabeel* or fountain and the ritual ablution pools near the Dome of the Rock where worshippers cleanse themselves before prayer. In Islamic and Jewish tradition the rivers of creation bubble up beneath the great Rock of the Noble Sanctuary. Throughout the Old City one sees beautiful but neglected Ottoman drinking fountains, set in ornate recesses tapping into resources deep below. Beneath the holy city excavations have revealed the imperative of water collection: north of the former temple area, where once stood the Antonia Fortress, the Struthion Pool, fed by subterranean aqueducts and by well-hewn Hasmonean water tunnels, can be seen under the Convent of Our Lady of Zion.

Across the land, wondrous aquifers, rocks saturated with water, hide deep below the surface, while the Sea of Galilee has itself become a reservoir; its receding water level symbolises very dramatically a major crisis facing Israel/Palestine—the desperate clamour for water. Jeremiah's ancient words seem so contemporary:

> Judah mourns
>   and her gates languish;
> they lie in gloom on the ground,
>   and the cry of Jerusalem goes up.
> Her nobles send their servants for water;
>   they come to the cisterns;

they find no water,
    they return with their vessels empty.
They are ashamed and dismayed
    and cover their heads,
because the ground is cracked.
    Because there has been no rain on the land
the farmers are dismayed;
    they cover their heads.

JEREMIAH 14:2–4

Throughout the scriptures, narratives relate the quest for underground water. For example, it is said of King Uzziah: 'He built towers in the wilderness and hewed out many cisterns, for he had large herds, both in the Shephelah and in the plain, and he had farmers and vine-dressers in the hills and in the fertile lands, for he loved the soil' (2 Chronicles 26:10). The prophet Isaiah rejoices: 'With joy you will draw water from the wells of salvation' (Isaiah 12:3). Jeremiah (2:13) laments: 'my people have committed two evils: they have forsaken me, the fountain of living water, and dug out cisterns for themselves, cracked cisterns that can hold no water.'

Spiritual resources

The search for water, and the imperative of collecting and guarding every precious drop, speaks to us of the necessity in our spiritual lives to build up reserves that we can turn to when it seems our well runs dry. Little by little we need to save up and conserve sources of inspiration that we can access when need be. Here we will consider four possible sources: from the biblical tradition (the Psalms); from the Catholic tradition, Benedictine wisdom for daily living; from the Orthodox tradition the great compendium of spiritual wisdom called the *Philokalia*, exemplified for us by Symeon the New Theologian and Maximos; from the evangelical tradition the hymns of Charles Wesley. Such writers will provide for us springs of hope to sustain the thirsty soul in the direst of times.

Songs of hope

The book of Psalms offers us an unfailing resource: we can turn to it whatever the emotion, whatever the situation we face. When we can't find words with which to pray, the Psalms become a reservoir of prayer we can tap. There are psalms to hearten and cheer us:

> As a deer longs for flowing streams,
>   so my soul longs for you, O God.
> My soul thirsts for God,
>   for the living God.
> When shall I come and behold
>   the face of God?
> My tears have been my food
>   day and night,
> while people say to me continually,
>   'Where is your God?'…
> Why are you cast down, O my soul,
>   and why are you disquieted within me?
> Hope in God; for I shall again praise him,
>   my help and my God.
>
> PSALM 42:1–3, 5–6

There are psalms that give voice to our deepest fears:

> Save me, O God, for the waters have come up to my neck.
> I sink in deep mire, where there is no foothold;
> I have come into deep waters, and the flood sweeps over me.
>
> PSALM 69:1–2

Others will inspire us: 'More majestic than the thunders of mighty waters, more majestic than the waves of the sea, majestic on high is the Lord!' (93:4). Others will reassure us of the presence with us of the God 'who turns the rock into a pool of water, the flint into a spring of water' (114:8).

Catholic reserves: tapping the wisdom of St Benedict

The *Rule of St Benedict* is a supreme example of wisdom literature: 'Listen carefully, my son, to the master's instructions, and attend to them with the ear of your heart. This is advice from a father who loves you...'[1]

In recent years, there have been fruitful encounters between the *Rule of Benedict* and family life[2] and between the text and the business world.[3] But how can a *Rule* one and a half thousand years old be relevant to Christian life in the 21st century? Chittister helpfully points out: '*Regula*, the word now translated to mean "rule", in the ancient sense meant "guidepost" or "railing", something to hang onto in the dark, something that points out the road, something that gives us support as we climb. The *Rule* of Benedict, in other words, is more wisdom than law.'[4]

Benedict's three vows

The triple vows of the *Rule* provide a framework to help us make sense of the sometimes conflicting dynamics of Christian discipleship today. We find ourselves caught between the pull of duty to others and the pull of developing the self, and the first two vows suggest a dialectic within which this tension can be not so much resolved, as held creatively.

Benedict's vow of *stability* commits the monk to stay with a particular community for life. It is the first of the vows, because it is about the total surrender of one's life to God, within the particular setting and context of a group of people. In a world where people are rushing around in ever greater degrees of mobility, this commitment invites us to reconsider a rootedness in the here and now, an attentiveness to the needs of a particular community, and firmly rejects the temptation that 'the grass is greener elsewhere'. The vow of *stabilitas* reminds us of the essentially incarnational nature of discipleship, and of the call to be fully present to a particular historical context. But this vow also calls us to consistency, to steadfastness, as Benedict puts it: 'to persevere in [our] stability' (58:9). It calls us to the rock of faithfulness and constancy in a sea of change and tempest of transition. In today's context, this vow is about not giving up, not giving way under the pressures which confront today's Christian, which include marginalisation and loss of respect in society. It is about rediscovering God's *hesed* or steadfast love and faithfulness, expressed in Paul's affirmation: 'I am sure that he who began a good work in you will bring it to completion' (Philippians 1:6, RSV).

Yet the biblical metaphors of 'standing in the evil day' (Ephesians 6) or 'remaining in the vine' (John 15) need also to be in conversation with the dynamic language of movement and motion with which Benedict both begins and ends his *Rule*:

> Run while you have the light of life.
> Prologue 13

> Run on the path of God's commandments.
> Prologue 49

> Hasten towards your heavenly home.
> 73:8

And so the vow of *stabilitas* stands in tension with Benedict's second vow of *conversatio morum*, the conversion of life, which calls for constant growth and change. This is an echo of scripture's call to *metanoia*, turning again to God, and resonates with Paul's resolve: 'Straining towards what is ahead' (Philippians 3:13).

Such a commitment can be both liberating and unnerving. It invites us to let go of cherished and familiar ways of working, to be ready for risk-taking, open to experimental and provisional patterns of witness and ministry which emerge as Christendom dissolves and the Church discovers different ways of being, in a post-Christian, postmodern world.[5] It calls us to accept the need for lifelong learning and continuous development. It requires of us both a thirst for fresh understanding of God's word and world, and also a vulnerability, a lowering of self-protective barriers, to be open to the God of surprises.

In his vow of *obedience* to Christ, as represented in the person of the abbot, Benedict is demanding the surrender of self-will, the giving up of any personal agenda, and the submission of the individual to the wider concerns of the community. The word 'obedience' comes from the Latin *ob audiens*, meaning 'to listen intently'. This vow calls for an undivided attentiveness to the will of God, represented in Gospel, *Rule*, and those set in authority: 'O that today you would listen to his voice! Do not harden your hearts' (Psalm 95:7–8). This attentive listening and discerning of God's will underpins and unites both the call to stability and the call to continuous conversion. Radically, it represents the primacy of God's will over any independent planning or prioritising in our ministries. It invites us to slow down, and to reach a place of acute theological reflection and prayer. In short, the triple vows cry out to us: stay at it, stay open, stay listening!

Handling paradoxes

It is this wisdom about holding together paradoxes and often conflicting demands that is the principal gift of the *Rule* to discipleship today. Benedict is emphatic about the use of time:

> Idleness is the enemy of the soul. Therefore, the brothers should have specified periods for manual labour as well as for prayerful reading. We believe that the times for both may be arranged as follows: From Easter to the first of October, they will spend their mornings after Prime till about the fourth hour at whatever work needs to be done. [Then] they will devote themselves to reading. But after Sext and their meal, they may rest on their beds in complete silence...
>
> **48:1–5**

There is a real danger today of burnout.[6] Time management is a pressing concern. Benedict calls his readers to live within an ordered rhythm of prayer, which celebrates the primacy of God and his resourcing in ministry. *Ora et labora*: he allows proper time for prayer, labour, study and creativity. Worship is to be considered the *Opus Dei*, the work of God. Benedict is emphatic: no one is to overwork. In an age where we find ourselves under intense pressures, here is a call to regain a sense of perspective. But it is not simply a question of managing time, but of living within the dialectic, within the tension of juggling different vocations or responsibilities at the same time. De Waal observes the message given by Benedictine Gothic architecture in the vault of a nave:

> Here is never-ending conflict. The high vaults strive to push the walls outwards; the flying buttresses strive to push them inwards. Here are columns, arches, walls all locked in unceasing combat… If there is a single reason why the Benedictine way of life has remained dynamic across the centuries, I suspect it is because the Rule carries within itself this same ability to hold together opposing forces, conflicting tensions.[7]

We can read a sense of balance revealed in the layout of a Benedictine monastery: there is the church, the chapter house, dormitory, refectory, kitchen… each reflecting different commitments and tasks, all held together by a common walkway, the cloister walk, and, at the centre of it all, the large open space of the cloister garden, where stands a spring or fountain. This speaks to every Christian of the need for living our lives not in fragmentedness but in connectedness, in unity and integrity: with a place of cleansing, refreshment and stillness at the very centre.

So Benedict's *Rule* can most powerfully shape discipleship today in its call to hold together disparate commitments within a creative tension: the call to community, the call to solitude; the desert and the city, the needs of body, mind and spirit; human decision-making and divine grace; standing still in stability and moving out in continuous conversion, and the balance between giving out and receiving from God. The *Rule* invites us to live with these tensions with a humble, vigilant and teachable heart (7). Benedict himself offers his *Rule* with such humility: 'Above all else we urge that if anyone finds this arrangement… unsatisfactory, he should arrange whatever he judges better' (18:22). We accept the *Rule* as a flexible tool, adaptable guidelines for daily living: a veritable reservoir of ancient but ever fresh wisdom.

Orthodox reserves: the *Philokalia*

The Philokalia (literally, 'love of the beautiful, the good') is a collection of texts written between the fourth and 15th centuries by spiritual masters of the Eastern Orthodox hesychast tradition. The collection was compiled in the 18th century by St Nikodemos of the Holy Mountain and St Makarios of Corinth. Translated into many languages, the book has become one of the major spiritual texts for Eastern Christians.

Symeon the New Theologian (949–1022) is one the Eastern Church's greatest mystics represented in the collection. He emphasises the necessity of personal encounter with the divine, and tells his own story:

He led me by the hand as one leads a blind man to the fountain head, that is, to the holy scriptures and to Your divine commandments… One day when I was hurrying to plunge myself in this daily bath, You met me on the road, You who had already drawn me out of the mire. Then for the first time the pure light of Your divine face shone before my weak eyes… From that day on, You returned often at the fountain source, You would plunge my head into the water, letting me see the splendour of your light… One day when it seemed as though You were plunging me over and over again in the lustral waters, lightning flashes surrounded me. I saw the rays from Your face merge with the waters; washed by these radiant waters, I was carried out of myself...[8]

For Symeon, the image of the waters becomes a powerful metaphor of the spiritual life, bespeaking the unfathomable resources of the Spirit, and God's generosity in sharing his gifts.[9] Symeon was based at Constantinople where, for 25 years, he was abbot of St Mamas monastery. He has been called in the East 'the greatest mystic of the Middle Ages', and was surnamed 'the New Theologian' by later admirers to identify him with such creative theologians as St John. He anticipated the later Byzantine hesychast movement with his teaching on personal communion with God in contemplation. His central conviction was that the Holy Spirit makes possible a conscious encounter with Christ and, in some sense, the vision of God in this life. In an age when doctrinal controversy divided the Greek and Latin churches—over the Western addition to the Nicean Creed 'We believe in the Holy Spirit, who proceeds from the Father *and the Son*'—Symeon taught that it is personal experience of the Spirit and God's kingdom which is paramount, within the eucharistic community of the Church.

Make no mistake! God is a fire, and has cast fire on the earth. The same Fire goes about looking for kindling to seize upon, for a ready disposition and will, in order to fall upon it and ignite it... when it has completely cleansed us of the filth of the passions, it becomes... light and joy without ceasing in us, and by participation, it makes us light ourselves. It is like a clay pot that has been set on the fire. At first it is somewhat blackened by the smoke of the burning fuel, but after the fuel has begun to burn fiercely, then it becomes all translucent and like the fire itself, and the smoke can communicate none of its blackness to it. Just so, indeed, does the soul which has begun to burn with divine longing see first of all the murk of its passions within it, billowing out like smoke in the fire of the Holy Spirit... After these things have been utterly destroyed... then the divine and immaterial fire unites itself essentially to the soul, too, and the latter is immediately kindled and becomes transparent, and shares in it like the clay pot does in the visible fire…

All the corrupting passions of sin vanish completely. The fruit of the Holy Spirit alone weighs heavy upon the soul, that fruit which is love, joy, peace, kindness, goodness, faith, meekness, humility, all-embracing continence, followed in succession and beauty by divine knowledge, the wisdom of the Word, and the abyss of Christ's hidden counsels and mysteries.[10]

What kind of divine knowledge can we seek? Maximos in the seventh century puts it in a text preserved in the *Philokalia*:

When the intellect (*nous*) practises contemplation, it advances in spiritual knowledge… the intellect is granted the grace of theology when, carried on wings of love… it is taken up into God and with the help of the Holy Spirit discerns—as far as this is possible for the human intellect—the qualities of God.[11]

Such knowledge is transforming: 'The intellect joined to God for long periods through prayer and love becomes wise, good, powerful, compassionate, merciful and long-suffering; in short, it includes with itself almost all the divine qualities.'[12]

Evangelical reserves: Charles Wesley

The brother of evangelist John Wesley, Charles wrote over 6000 hymns which have been at the heart of evangelical spirituality. They combine rich theology with personal experience and lead the user to thirst for a deeper encounter with God's grace. Wesley celebrates the personal indwelling of the Holy Spirit, the sanctifying work of the Holy Spirit and the all-sufficiency of Christ. In 'And can it be' he rejoices in Christ's liberating power:

Long my imprisoned spirit lay
Fast bound in sin and nature's night;
Thine eye diffused a quick'ning ray,
I woke, the dungeon flamed with light;
My chains fell off, my heart was free;
I rose, went forth and followed Thee.

Wesley's hymns inspire a renewed confidence in God in times of trial:

Thou hidden source of calm repose,
thou all-sufficient love divine,
my help and refuge from my foes,
secure I am if thou art mine;
and lo! from sin and grief and shame
I hide me, Jesus, in thy name…

Jesus, my all in all thou art,
my rest in toil, my ease in pain,
the medicine of my broken heart,
in war my peace, in loss my gain,
my smile beneath the tyrant's frown,
in shame my glory and my crown.

In want my plentiful supply,
in weakness my almighty power,
in bonds my perfect liberty,
my light in Satan's darkest hour,
in grief my joy unspeakable,
my life in death, my heaven in hell.

His hymn 'Let us plead for faith alone' reveals unshakable trust in Christ, the unmovable Rock:

Let us for this faith contend,
sure salvation is the end;
heaven already is begun,
everlasting life is won.

Only let us persevere
till we see our Lord appear,
never from the Rock remove,
saved by faith which works by love.

Perhaps his best loved composition is a hymn that we return to again and again in times of doubt or distress:

Jesus, lover of my soul, let me to Thy bosom fly,
While the nearer waters roll, while the tempest still is high.
Hide me, O my Saviour, hide, till the storm of life is past;
Safe into the haven guide; O receive my soul at last.

Other refuge have I none, hangs my helpless soul on Thee;
Leave, ah! leave me not alone, still support and comfort me.
All my trust on Thee is stayed, all my help from Thee I bring;
Cover my defenceless head with the shadow of Thy wing…

Plenteous grace with Thee is found, grace to cover all my sin;
Let the healing streams abound; make and keep me pure within.
Thou of life the fountain art, freely let me take of Thee;
Spring Thou up within my heart; rise to all eternity.

An overflowing reservoir…

In Ezekiel's vision (chapter 47), an underground stream feeding the cistern or container of the water by the threshold of the temple is overflowing:

Then he brought me back to the entrance of the temple; there, water was flowing from below the threshold of the temple towards the east (for the temple faced east); and the water was flowing down from below the south end of the threshold of the temple, south of the altar. Then he brought me out by way of the north gate, and led me round on the outside to the outer gate that faces towards the east; and the water was coming out on the south side.

EZEKIEL 47:1–2

Ezekiel's vision expands: a spring of God's generous blessing bursts forth from under the altar of the temple and it spills out to bring renewal to the whole world. The water gets deeper and deeper as Ezekiel follows the line of the river from the holy city out and out into the deserts. At first the prophet can wade in the water, but soon it comes up right to his waist, so he must swim in the river of God's blessing! And others can jump in, too! Let's not hoard the reserves we discover, but share them.

Questions for reflection

1 Which of the psalms do you return to again and again, as an important element in your own reservoir?
2 As you reflect on the wisdom of Benedict, what paradoxes can you identify in your own spiritual experience?
3 Symeon wrote: 'You were plunging me over and over again in the lustral waters.' What is your experience of the Holy Spirit?
4 What is your favourite Wesley hymn? Why? In what way can it become a resource in prayer that you can go back to?
5 What spiritual writers or prayers would you want to include in your reservoir or cistern of spiritual resources?

Prayer exercise

Either
On a clean piece of paper draw a circle to represent your life. Divide it up into different sized segments representing the proportions of time you normally spend on tasks and commitments. Reflect on whether there is a right balance between work and play, prayer and activity (this can be done in pairs in a group). Do you maintain such a balance and perspective in your life, juggling the demands of work, recreation and home? Notice the tension between possible fragmentedness and the wholeness of the circle. Close by placing the papers under a cross as a sign of surrendering our often frantic lives to the Lordship of Christ.

Or
Make a review of the last 24 hours. Reflect on how you used your time. Where was God in all this? How did you handle interruptions or unexpected challenges? Did you find yourself resenting any task? Be penitent for negative attitudes or opportunities missed. Praise God for the times you were aware of his presence.

5

Tunnelling beneath the rock: developing communications

Voices echo beneath us, ricocheting off the walls of the chambers. Excited cries reverberate and resonate; gentle sighs penetrate the stillness. Is that a tapping sound we can hear—is someone trying to make contact? We are exploring here the theme of communicating underground: the vocabulary of prayer, languages of the soul. Questions for reflection in this chapter are included in the text, so you can pause to get your breath back along the way!

From the most ancient times right up to the present day, tunnels in the Holy Land tell the story of communication and transit. Today's visitor to the excavations of the City of David in Jerusalem can see tunnels used by David's envoys when he took the city from the Jebusites in about 1000BC. The story told in 2 Samuel 5:6–10 relates the climbing up of hidden water shafts to attack the 'stronghold of Zion'. His men crawled up through a cave system hollowed out by flowing water and so infiltrated the city. The water conduit enabled the stealthy access to the city: we imagine the conquerors shouting down to David's people: 'We made it!' This tunnel, just wide enough for one person to squeeze through, was discovered by Dr Eilat Mazar in 2008. Together with the Warren's Shaft and other passageways, it forms a labyrinth of tunnels beneath the original part of the holy city. Not far away, it is possible for the pilgrim to walk through the recently excavated Western Wall Tunnel deep below the old city, which follows the foundations of Herod's rebuilding of the temple area. Nearby, and accessible only to Muslim worshippers, steps near the Dome of the Rock lead down to a vast underground complex popularly known as 'Solomon's Stables'—a series of vaulted arches supported by 88 pillars: a space of 18,000 square feet built by Herod the Great to support the platform of the Temple Mount, now used as a Muslim prayer hall.

In ancient times, local peoples living in caves throughout the Holy Land depended on underground passages for communications; many caves interconnected with each other by means of passages, vital in a time of invasion or threat. Anthropologist Dr Ali Qleibo reports: 'The passages between the caves are often narrow. One would have to stoop down, crawl, and at times squeeze oneself between the small apertures connecting the caves.'[1] In contemporary times tunnels in the Holy Land open up new possibilities for communication. Several tunnels have been blasted through hillsides for the new high-speed railway between Tel Aviv and Jerusalem. To the west of the city, high-tech companies in Jerusalem's 'Silicon Valley' are at the cutting edge of technological research and development, pioneering, for example, fibre-optic cables to be laid underground, and other advances in telecommunications. Pipelines are sunk beneath the surface throughout the land, carrying water, fuels and communications. We are aware, too, of the tunnels between Egypt and the Gaza Strip at Rafah, used to smuggle into the territory foodstuffs and even cars; for the imprisoned residents, a vital if illegal route for communications of all kinds.

Learning the language of the soul

The spiritual explorer needs to learn the art of communication not only with the divine but also about discoveries about the divine. How can we describe to others what is happening to us on our spiritual journey? How can we depict, for the benefit of ourselves and for others, the spiritual road that we are taking: experiences of prayer, transitions that we travel through, impediments that we face? How can we find images for the intangible, 'naming' the invisible, bringing to visualisation the unseen; expressing the silences? How can we externalise into words the interior emotions and movements in the soul? How can we learn spiritual fluency?

We find ourselves lost for words, tongue-tied, dumbfounded, longing to find an expression. As Barry and Connolly put it:

> ... most people are inarticulate when they try... to describe their deeper feelings and attitudes. They can be even less articulate when they try to describe their relationship with God... For to begin to talk about this aspect of their lives requires the equivalent of a new language, the ability to articulate inner experience.[2]

In the 16th century Francisco de Osuna wrote: 'some matters of mystical theology cannot be understood in ordinary language.'[3] The Franciscan writer composed three *Spiritual Alphabets* which introduced the seeker to key ways of approaching the passion, spiritual disciplines and the practice of prayer. As Giles explains: 'We must become as little children, learning our ABCs of spirituality.'[4]

We need to develop *spiritual literacy*. We need to be able to read our soul. We need to access appropriate vocabulary for spirituality: images and pictures, often stunning and unnerving, which help us describe and clarify what is happening to us; language and terms that will develop our awareness, and make the abstract concrete, make transparent what is opaque, cloudy. We need interpretive frameworks. We need to develop proficiency in the use of appropriate language, linguistic competency, both for speaking with God himself, and for sharing our experiences with others.

Where can we encounter the raw material of a divine–human relationship described by others? In what places might we find accounts of people's experience of prayer? How can we encounter the experiences of others? There is a wide range of genres, both traditional and contemporary. Historic and classic sources include treatises, sermons, devotional manuals, pastoral and spiritual direction handbooks, discourses of spiritual direction, spiritual autobiography or personal history, journals or reflection on experience. Other sources to be mined include monastic rules, stories and narratives, letters of spiritual direction, poems, ritual/liturgical texts, and the whole range of art and music.

But we need also to relate to the culture of our time and place—connecting with contemporary images that speak powerfully in our own context. Carolyn Gratton puts it: 'A spiritual guide needs to be a skilled translator. People need to have guidance in the language of their own actual life state, whether they are academics or steelworkers, teenagers or senior citizens.'[5]

Communications in the Holy Land can give us clues. There we encounter both inscriptions in ancient language from the past, and the latest examples of today's communication explosion. So we need to access language new and old. Like the householder of the kingdom, we bring out of our storeroom treasures both old and new (Matthew 13:52). But Joseph Campbell cautions: 'We must remember, however, that the metaphors of one historically conditioned period, and the symbols they innervate, may not speak to the persons who are living long after that historical moment.'[6] We need to be alert to contemporary sources which connect us with the experience of young people, and learn their arresting images in song books, worship texts, guides to spiritual life, noticing also what metaphors emerge in today's movies and technology.

Sandra Schneiders, too, reminds us of the importance of context in shaping religious language appropriate to the time and place.[7] Nevertheless, many of the biblical and traditional metaphors of the spiritual life turn out to be archetypal and resonate with our souls across the centuries and cultures.[8]

Ancient vocabulary:
five types of biblical language

The questions I suggest here can help us unlock language which can be employed effectively in conversations and witness with spiritual searchers and enquirers.

1 Tender and daring language of friends and lovers

Familial, relational language and metaphors of tenderness and risk open up great avenues for exploring one's relationship with God. The prophets show us the way:

> You have seduced me, Yahweh,
>   and I have let myself be seduced.
> JEREMIAH 20:7, NJB

> I am going to lure her
>   And lead her out into the wilderness
>   And speak to her heart.
> HOSEA 2:14, JB

This is taken to depths of a longing, passionate love in the sensuality of the Song of Songs. Though this collection of love poems does not mention God, the divine presence is energising the relationship. The Song not only uses erotic language, it also develops the theme of hide and seek, the presence and absence of the lover, so the emotions of both communion and distress are explored. It moves from lines like: 'You have ravished my heart, my sister, my bride, you have ravished my heart with a glance of your eyes' (4:9), to 'I sought him, but did not find him; I called him, but he gave no answer' (5:6).

- How would you describe your relationship with God? What are your primary metaphors?
- How do you feel about using the language of intimacy with God? Are you comfortable or uncomfortable about this? Why?

- 'My true love hath my heart and I have his' (Philip Sidney). For whom might this language be appropriate and for whom might it be inappropriate?

2 Energising language of pilgrims and travellers

Geographical and topographical metaphors resonate and unpack the great contemporary theme of the spiritual journey. There are different threads we could pursue: the experience of spiritual exile, drifting, lostness and homecoming; our own journey into freedom, echoing exodus and paschal imagery. We might explore the experience of passing through storms and chaos, of voyaging into the deep. The image of the roadway or pilgrimage to God invites us to identify barriers and impediments to our progress. We can identify phases in the journey and get a sense of our bearings, considering the direction to which God is summoning us next. These sorts of questions emerge:

- What is your experience of encountering the unexpected on your spiritual journey? Did this lead you to conversion or to change?
- In the book of Isaiah God says: 'remove every obstruction from my people's way' (57:14) and 'build up the highway, clear it of stones' (62:10). What impediments to your spiritual progress can you name? What roadblocks do you need to overcome if you are to advance in the spiritual journey?
- Can you identify any ways in which you are becoming sidetracked or tempted to 'go off at a tangent' from your spiritual path?

3 Adventurous language of explorers and seekers

Within the contours of the spiritual landscape, we encounter features representing key aspects of the prayer journey. In our explorations, we traverse the desert, ascend the mountain, cross the bridge and descend to the cave. We are invited to become fearless adventurers, explorers of the spiritual terrain. This imagery beckons us forwards towards risky places in our spiritual odyssey, summoning us to curiosity and fresh discoveries. We can explore the desert of the soul:

our experience of emptiness, openness, loneliness. We can encourage a scaling of the heights: conceiving the spiritual journey as a climb up the mountain—a spirituality of ascent. In this book we are plumbing the depths, exploring themes of darkness, the cave of the heart.

- How does the language of explorers reverberate in your own soul?
- Recall a phase in your spiritual journey that felt like passing through a desert. What positive aspects there can you now name?
- Which image are you more drawn to: climbing the mountain or plumbing the depths? Can you say why?
- Which aspects of the spiritual landscape are you discovering now? What new discoveries have you made in the last year?
- How helpful do you find the language of being 'an explorer of the interior space'? What does it suggest to you about the terrain of the spiritual life?

4 Creative language of builders and citizens

We do not need to look to the heavens for spiritual imagery; it is close at hand. We can explore the inner spaces expressed in spatial, urban, domestic and architectural metaphors. Complementing the dynamic imagery of journey and pilgrimage, the biblical and Christian tradition beckons us to metaphors celebrating the divine seeking residence in human lives: we can communicate truths in the spiritual life through the picture language of the building and the city, the temple, house, castle. This also opens up for us the language of spiritual imprisonment, crossing thresholds and opening doors.

- What are you aiming at? What are your plans? What do you hope will be your lasting legacy? Recall Hebrews 11:10: '[Abraham] looked forward to the city that has foundations, whose architect and builder is God.' Recall Psalm 127:1: 'Unless the Lord builds the house, those who build it labour in vain.'
- In what ways does your spiritual life resemble a construction site? Are there things that need to be torn down, before something new emerges?

- Is there any sense in your spiritual life that you have become trapped or restricted in some way? How does the imagery of opening doors or finding release resonate with your longings? Is there something in you that needs to be unlocked? Do you feel in any way 'fastened up' or 'zipped up' spiritually?

5 Sensuous language of body and soul

While the Hebrew scriptures declare that creation is 'very good', the Christian faith affirms that the divine Word became enfleshed, embodied, taking on human flesh and blood in the person of Jesus Christ. In the wake of the incarnation, physicality and spirituality become inseparable. This enables us to develop a Christian anthropology that takes seriously both the human body and our capacity to welcome the divine, as we are made in the image and likeness of God (Genesis 1:27). We encounter striking physical images. In the tenth century Symeon the New Theologian wrote of the need for one to have 'purified his heart through repentance and many tears, and penetrated the depths of humility, and became pregnant with the Holy Spirit, by the grace and love for mankind of our Lord Jesus Christ'.[9]

The physicality of the body can open up for us conversations about the heart, the spiritual senses, feeding, inebriation, spiritual nakedness, hurting/healing and heaviness/lightness.

- How comfortable are you in using physical and visceral images to speak of the spiritual life?
- What is your experience of being wounded by God?
- What do you understand by the idea that in prayer we become 'fully alive'?
- How would you develop the theme of spiritual thirst and hunger to describe your own experience of finding God? 'Taste and see that the Lord is good' (Psalm 34:8). What does God taste like for you? Then look up Psalm 119:103 for one response to this.
- '"Come," my heart says, "seek his face!" Your face, Lord, do I seek'

(Psalm 27:8). How would you describe the face of God, as you experience God in your prayer?

This is an invitation to deeper prayer, for as Fischer observes:

> Integrating a new image into prayer is a different process from analyzing its adequacy from a theological perspective… The process of integrating new images into our spiritual lives involves not only talking about new metaphors, but praying to God under these new names, seeing self and world through these images… a symbol or image achieves power in the spiritual life by gradually unfolding its significance…[10]

Contemporary language: Five types of lingo in a technological age

Today's world, dominated by information technology and digital gadgetry, suggests many images and metaphors that can be used in spiritual conversations. Language is making a transition: icons and fonts are not what they used to be! The Internet search engine becomes a symbol of humanity's quest for answers, and a preoccupation with 'surfing the net' reveals the restlessness of the human heart: 'googling' is a contemporary preoccupation. We note five transitions in the recent use of language, raising penetrating questions about our spiritual life.

1 Identity: from authenticity to artificiality

The development of computers mirrors the human soul: in the past we spoke of being made in God's image—today we realise that we are 'hardwired' for God. Moore and Gillette, for example, comment that archetypes are the 'hard-wired components of our genetically transmitted psychic machine'.[11] The hard drive of our being is designed for communication with God: this is a basic fact of our human 'operating system'.

Our basic identity is rooted in a realisation that each person is a child of God, uniquely gifted and cherished by God. But modern technology can not only depersonalise us so we become an anonymous consumer, it can also lead to a dichotomy between 'online' and 'offline' personalities. We can create 'digital alter egos', and sites urge us to 'create a platform'. We can choose our own 'avatar' symbol to represent us in a chat room. Identities can be falsified. There are massive dangers of superficiality and deception in Internet use, and people can end up living in a virtual world, not in reality. Encryption and decoding may speak of the need for secrecy or represent a cover-up. Pseudonyms and nicknames may represent a need to conceal gender or age. In the passion for taking 'selfies' one can choose the background and those to be pictured with, and as in Photoshop, one can alter details at will. The spiritual autobiography of the past has given way to Facebook pages and one's (edited) personal profile. Privacy 'in private browsing' can either be safeguarding a sense of personal respect or be a cloak for mischief![12]

All this has tremendous potential for helping us explore real issues in spiritual life. Since Adam, we have been tempted to hide from God, but as David came to realise in his penitential psalm:

> You desire truth in the inward being;
>   therefore, teach me wisdom in my secret heart.
> PSALM 51:6

The basic questions remain:

- Who am I? How can I be my true, authentic self? Is there any place for wearing different personas or masks with God?
- How transparent and honest can you be with God; would you put your 'cam' on, as it were, so you can reveal the expressions in your face?

2 Belonging: from communion to connectivity and social networking

One priority of our times is the constant desire to be connected to the Internet and to reach out across cyberspace. If we are not able to be connected, we cannot take part in any form of electronic communication. Having a WiFi connection is key. We must get 'online'—plug in, switch on, log in. Spirits sink when we get the message 'Your browser is not responding'. We hate it when 'the system crashes', the computer runs 'slow' or the mobile phone signal breaks up. We need to be properly tuned and have our personal settings just right or things won't work. Useful and resonant metaphors emerge here. Connectivity is the basic essential. Using a mobile phone reminds us that God can call at any time or place, but we can be switched off or be in sleep mode! A minister said to me recently about listening to God: 'Prayer is about tuning in to God's wavelength, not making a broadcast from one's own station.'

In the past we spoke of our relationships with God and one another in terms of spiritual communion within the mystical body of Christ. Today we speak of relating by participating in social networks. We are urged to get 'linked in'. We belong to a 'virtual community'; we may have many contacts called 'friends', but such so-called friendship may be a mile wide and an inch deep. This prompts challenging questions:

- What is friendship—with others, with God?
- How do you express your relationship with the divine?
- What sustains your connectivity and communication with God?

3 Communicating: from talking/listening to God to 'instant messaging' / downloads

The acquisition of information or data is one of today's imperatives. While the Book of Common Prayer spoke of 'hearing and receiving God's holy Word', this priority may today be translated into the language of downloading God's word into our hearts.

Today, as we download apps, articles, movies, YouTube clips and music, we remind ourselves that we actually need to do something about the download; otherwise it simply clutters the space in our memory devices.

Communication lies at the heart of the culture of the Internet. Where in the past we offered 'arrow prayers', like 'Make haste to help me, O Lord' (Psalm 38:22), today people talk of instant messaging and tweeting God. There is a need for immediate gratification or response—we do not like to wait: speed matters. Pressure on time is an issue; one priest said to me recently, 'I text God, not write a letter.' 'Tweets to God' may convey the sense that God is available and interested in our goings-on, or may trivialise our life, so we miss the bigger spiritual issues. Referring to an online video call, a recent spiritual writer asks: 'Is it fanciful to see that electronic realm which brought our son almost literally before us as an analogy of the spiritual realm through which God brings himself before us, so that we could say prayer is akin to Skyping?'[13] These questions emerge:

- How fulsome or generous is your communication with God?
- Do you 'tweet' in briefest mode, or can you linger in an untimed encounter?
- Is there anything you can't say to God?
- To what extent do you experience a real exchange with God—a two-way communication?

4 Reflecting: from journaling to blogging

Individualism and self-preoccupation within a narcissistic postmodern culture reveals itself in the need some have to 'blog', replacing the slower, reflective, handwritten journaling of old. There is a shift from reference to 'affections' to the declaration of feelings; a movement from facts to experience, from 'the' story to 'my' story; and emoticons can be inserted into messages to symbolise current states of mind. Ask yourself:

- How do you reflect on your life?
- What disciplines or methods do you build into your life to ensure regular periods for theological reflection?

5 Expressing: from sin and worship to virus and awe

Today people express a worshipful or reverent attitude when they express their gratefulness for inventiveness, and appreciation of contemporary design, ergonomics, and technological breakthroughs. Words like 'cool', 'magic' and 'wicked' form part of daily vocabulary. There has been the rediscovery of the use of the word 'awesome'. Outmoded and unpopular concepts like 'sin' might be conveyed through the imagery of being infected with a virus, cyber attacks or bombardment, things going viral. There is a diversity of images and metaphors that can be used in exploring our spirituality.

- What words or images would you use to express your feelings towards God?
- What images of God are you comfortable with?
- What imagery or metaphor do you use to express the traditional concepts of penitence and wonder?

There is the risk of consumerist detachment replacing real engagement. There is much talk—and less walk: too much information, too little formation. The imperative is to connect with the culture and notice images that might illuminate our understanding of the spiritual life and equip us for its expression.

Prayer exercise

Write a letter in which you explain to a friend why you are a Christian or a seeker. Use appropriate, arresting metaphors and figures of speech that you sense have the potential to open up a fruitful exchange.

6

Plummeting into the abyss: descending into the depths of God

We are filled with a strange mixture of excitement and apprehension. Adrenaline courses through our veins and hope quickens our heartbeat. We sense we might be on the brink of a great discovery, but we also feel ourselves teetering on the edge of a subterranean precipice. We sense we might lose our footing and hurtle without control into the shadows. We experience a kind of spiritual vertigo as we stand on the brink of a bottomless pit. We're standing on a ledge and feel we might plummet into the darkness below at any moment. We are initially aghast at the chasm below us: an eerie, inky blackness. We can't make anything out. It is awesome, fearful, yet strangely inviting. We feel drawn, summoned into depths that will be impossible to navigate.

There is an intoxicating magnetic power calling us to penetrate the mysterious caverns and galleries. Dare we take a leap in the dark and dive far below? Can you let go of your grip and allow yourself to tumble? A sense of suspense dawns in our hearts: we have pounding hearts and sweaty palms! Are we ready for astonishing discoveries of God that will be impossible to put into words? Are we prepared to become awestruck, dumbfounded? In this chapter we are led into a luminous darkness with the help of Gregory of Nyssa, Dionysius, the Rhineland mystics and Angela of Foligno.

At the top of the Mount of Olives hides the cave in which Jesus sat with his disciples Peter, James, John and Andrew (Mark 13:3) when he revealed to them the mysteries concerning the destruction of Jerusalem and the end of the world (related in Matthew 24, Mark

13 and Luke 21, the so-called 'Olivet Discourse'). Located near the summit of the mountain, it would have been a secluded and sheltered place for a small group to gather to receive the revelations or *apocalyptis*.

In the early fourth century, Eusebius wrote in his *Demonstration of the Gospel* (6:18):

> According to the common and received account, the feet of our Lord and Saviour truly stood upon the Mount of Olives at the cave that is shown there. On the ridge of the Mount of Olives He prayed and handed on to His disciples the mysteries of the end, and after this He made His ascension into heaven.

In his *Life of Constantine* (3:43), Eusebius calls it a 'mystic cave': 'Indeed a true report holds the Saviour to have initiated His disciples into secret mysteries in this very cave.' Above it, Constantine's mother Helena built her Eleona basilica in AD336 and it became a great place of pilgrimage and reflection. Today, the Carmelite Pater Noster Church stands nearby, celebrating the gift of the Lord's Prayer.

Far below, in the depths of the Kidron Valley, two caves draw us deeper into a sense of wonderment. The 'Grotto of Gethsemane', as it is called, is approached through a corridor cut into the hillside at the foot of the Mount of Olives. This cave was often frequented by Jesus— he loved to go to the stillness of Gethsemane; Luke tells us it was 'his custom' (Luke 22:39) and John tells us 'Jesus often met there with his disciples' (John 18:2). Scholars believe it was not only a site of teaching and fellowship but was also the place of the arrest of Jesus.[1]

Nearby, one descends over 80 steps from the Kidron Valley to the Tomb of Mary, a cavernous underground church. Down, down, down goes the pilgrim, and one's eyes get accustomed to the dimness. Mary's empty sepulchre looms up in the darkness at its deepest point, confronting the pilgrim with the inexplicable mystery of her dormition and translation to the heights of heaven from the deeps.

Opposite, across the valley, the Dome of the Rock, atop the Ophel Ridge, protects the great Rock Cave which lies beneath its resplendent canopy. In the Islamic tradition, a mysterious cave below the great stony outcrop is known as 'the well of souls', while in Jewish tradition, the Talmud teaches that the Rock of Moriah is the earth's foundation stone marking the centre of the world and serves as a cover for the abyss containing the raging waters of the flood. The Muslim tradition also holds that beneath the great Rock is located a bottomless pit with the flowing waters of paradise underneath.

In the far north of the Holy Land Christians ponder the identity of Jesus at Caesarea Philippi, where he asked: 'Who do people say that I am?' (Mark 8:27). Jesus invited contemplation of this mystery precisely at the mystical cave of Banias, where in Greco-Roman times it was believed that the half-goat, half-man deity Pan dwelt. Josephus writes:

> The place is called Panium, where is a top of a mountain that is raised to an immense height, and at its side, beneath, or at its bottom, a dark cave opens itself; within which there is a horrible precipice, that descends abruptly to a vast depth; it contains a mighty quantity of water, which is immovable; and when anybody lets down anything to measure the depth of the earth beneath the water, no length of cord is sufficient to reach it.[2]

Pilgrims visit the site today to reflect on the very mystery of Christ. Such mystic caves represent the enigmatic workings of God, his hidden purposes, often unfathomable and unsearchable: 'We speak God's wisdom, secret and hidden... the Spirit searches everything, even the depths of God' (1 Corinthians 2:7, 10). The darkness of the cave speaks to us of the mystery of God. God is always beyond our best concepts and categories, and human language cannot communicate his wonder. We can move beyond words to the prayer of dumbfounded amazement. This is the apophatic tradition, the *via negativa*: we come to the point where we admit the limits of our language when attempting to speak of God. The question posed to Job confronts us too: 'Can you find out the deep things of God? Can you find out the limit of the Almighty?... Deeper than Sheol—what can you know?' (11:7–8). Isaiah confesses: 'Truly, you are a God who hides himself' (Isaiah 45:15). With Paul we say: 'O the depth of the riches and wisdom and knowledge of God! How unsearchable are his judgements and how inscrutable his ways!' (Romans 11:33).

Mystery becomes a key word

Seven times, the writer of the letter to the Ephesians employs the word 'mystery':

- 'he has made known to us the mystery of his will, according to his good pleasure that he set forth in Christ' (1:9)
- 'the mystery was made known to me by revelation' (3:3)
- 'perceive my understanding of the mystery of Christ' (3:4)
- 'In former generations this mystery was not made known to humankind, as it has now been revealed to his holy apostles and prophets by the Spirit' (3:5)
- 'make everyone see what is the plan of the mystery hidden for ages in God who created all things' (3:9)
- 'This is a great mystery, and I am applying it to Christ and the church' (5:32)
- 'Pray also for me, so that when I speak, a message may be given to me to make known with boldness the mystery of the gospel' (6:19)

The letter to the Colossians, in similar vein, marvels at 'the mystery that has been hidden throughout the ages and generations but has now been revealed to his saints' (1:26). The writer speaks of 'the riches of the glory of this mystery, which is Christ in you, the hope of glory' (1:27). He prays that his readers will gain 'the riches of assured understanding and have the knowledge of God's mystery, that is, Christ himself' (2:2). The mystic writers explore this theme through the image of darkness, but as Matthews cautions us, this summons us to a different mindset, and an expansion of our normal patterns of thought:

> We have become used to thinking of the Christian faith in terms of the light that it provides, the illumination that it gives to the mind and soul. To understand it as a step into darkness requires a different frame of mind, a change of attitude for which we are little prepared.[3]

We are also summoned to discover fresh images of God. We are so used to thinking of a God 'up there' or 'out there', a God remote enough not to disturb us! Sometimes this goes with Sunday school images of an old man with a beard or a judging schoolmaster god looking down on us with a scowl on his face. In a dualistic perspective that opposes the divine and human, God is seen as transcendent, beyond the world. But now, we are invited to discover God within, below, beneath. As Fox puts it: 'To relocate divinity in the depths of nature and of the self is to re-encourage an entire civilization to listen to its creative powers and to allow those powers to emerge once again. Divinity most emerges from the depths…'[4]

Gregory of Nyssa: encounter divine darkness

Gregory of Nyssa (335–94) was the first writer to develop this message through the image of darkness; it was to become an important strand in thinking of spiritual development throughout the history of Christian spirituality. Danielou puts it: 'In Gregory of Nyssa… the term "darkness" takes on a new meaning and an essentially mystical connotation… Gregory's originality consists in the fact that he was the first to express this characteristic of the highest stages of mystical experience.'[5] His *Life of Moses*, a map of the Christian pilgrimage as it is suggested to him by the exodus accounts, culminates in the ascent of the mountain of divine knowledge, represented by Sinai. Gregory claims that an integral element of the Christian pilgrimage is the encounter with divine darkness:

For leaving behind everything that is observed, not only what sense comprehends but also what the intelligence thinks it sees, it keeps on penetrating deeper until by the intelligence's yearning for understanding it gains access to the invisible and the incomprehensible, and there it sees God. This is the true knowledge of what is sought; this is the seeing that consists in not seeing, because that which is sought transcends all knowledge, being separated on all sides by incomprehensibility as by a kind of darkness. Wherefore John the sublime, who penetrated into the luminous darkness, says, 'No one has ever seen God', thus asserting that knowledge of the divine essence is unattainable not only by men and women but also by every intelligent creature.

When, therefore, Moses grew in knowledge, he declared that he had seen God in the darkness, that is, that he had then come to know that what is divine is beyond all knowledge and comprehension, for the text says, 'Moses approached the dark cloud where God was.' What God? He who 'made darkness his hiding place,' as David says, who also was initiated into the mysteries in the same inner sanctuary.[6]

In Moses' first encounter with God, in the burning bush, God appears as light, as illumination. For Gregory, this represents the beginning of Christian conversion, a turning from the darkness of falsehood to the light of Christ. This process of illumination, for beginners, involves a purification of the soul from foreign elements. However, as the Christian, like Moses, progresses along the spiritual journey, he or she is led into darkness: not a negative darkness but a 'luminous darkness'. This represents the unknowability of God: this is the apophatic spiritual path, which falls silent before the unspeakable mystery of God. Danielou puts it:

After learning all that can be known of God, the soul discovers the limits of this knowledge; and this discovery is an advance, because now there is an awareness of the divine transcendence and incomprehensibility. We have then arrived at a negative, 'apophatic' theology. For we have now an authentic experience, a true vision. And the darkness is a positive reality that helps us to know God—that is why it is called luminous. For it implies an awareness of God that transcends all determination, and thus it is far truer than any determined categorical knowledge. For here in this obscurity the soul experiences the transcendence of the divine nature, that infinite distance by which God surpasses all creation.[7]

Andrew Louth explains: 'It is an experience beyond the senses and beyond the intellect; it is a feeling awareness of a fragrance that delights and enraptures the soul.'[8]

Dionysius: leave everything behind

In the fifth century, the writer known as Dionysius develops the thought of Gregory:

the mysteries of God's Word
lie simple, absolute and unchangeable
in the brilliant darkness of a hidden silence.

Amid the deepest shadow
they pour overwhelming light
on what is most manifest.

Amid the wholly unsensed and unseen
they completely fill our sightless minds
with treasures beyond all beauty.[9]

He continues, 'As we plunge into that darkness which is beyond intellect, we shall find ourselves not simply running short of words but actually speechless and unknowing.'[10]

Dionysius echoes the thought of Gregory of Nyssa; indeed, he seems to have known his *Life of Moses*—he too uses a similar image to explore the significance of darkness. Thus he writes:

> Leave behind you everything perceived and understood, everything perceptible and understandable, all that is not and all that is, and, with your understanding laid aside, strive upward as much as you can toward union with him who is beyond all being and knowledge. By an undivided and absolute abandonment of yourself and everything… you will be uplifted to the ray of the divine shadow which is above everything that is.[11]

Within his Christianised Neoplatonism, Dionysius finds the apex of the spiritual search.[12]

The Rhineland mystics: risk going deeper

The Rhineland region of Germany and neighbouring areas witnessed a remarkable flowering of mysticism in the 14th century, especially among the Dominicans. Some trace links to Hildegard of Bingen, but the main representatives were Eckhart and Tauler, while the Beguines—a lay women's movement—are represented by Hadewijch of Brabant and Maechthild of Magdeburg. All share a rich understanding of the depths of God and delight in underground imagery.

Meister Eckhart: allow yourself to sink

The German mystic and theologian Eckhart (1260–1328) taught that the *via positiva*, delighting in vivid metaphors and images, needs to be complemented by the apophatic way, the *via negativa*: we need to go beyond images, because they are only a starting point. Eckhart affirmed: 'the freer you are from images the more receptive you are to his interior operation.'[13] Eckhart invites us to discover the depths:

Think of the soul as a vortex or a whirlpool
  And you will understand how we are to
Sink
   eternally
     from negation
       to negation
         into the one.
And how we are to
Sink
   eternally
     from letting go
       to letting go
         into God.[14]

Delighting in the imagery of sea and lake, he goes on:

The highest work of God is compassion.
  And this means that God sets the soul
in the highest and purest place which it can occupy:
in space,
in the sea,
in a fathomless ocean,
and there
God works compassion.[15]

Johannes Tauler: discover a hidden abyss in yourself

A disciple of Eckhart, Tauler (1300–61), in a sermon to prepare for the Feast of Pentecost and the coming of the Holy Spirit, writes about our human capacity and receptivity for the divine. True prayer, he says, is

So that God may in reality enter into the purest, most inward, noblest part of the soul—its deepest ground... the soul has a hidden abyss, untouched by time and space, which is far superior to anything that gives life and movement to the body. Into this noble and wondrous ground... there descends that bliss of which we have spoken. Here the soul has its eternal abode. Here a man (sic) becomes so still and essential, so single-minded... for God himself is present in this noble realm, and works and reigns within.

But this capacity to welcome in one's depths the divine Spirit is not only for one's own private edification or fulfilment. Rather, it enables a big-heartedness that intercedes for all in need of any kind:

They draw all into their embrace in this same abyss, in this fire of love, as in a divine contemplation. Then they turn their gaze back to this loving abyss, to this fire of love, and there they rest; and after plunging into it, they descend to all who are in want until they return to the loving, dark, silent rest of the abyss.

There is an ebb and flow of prayer and action:

Thus they go in and out, and yet remain at all times within, in this sweet, silent ground in which they have their substance and life, in which they move and have their being. Wherever one finds such men, one finds nothing but divine life. Their conduct, their actions, their whole manner of life is divinized. They are noble souls, and the whole of Christendom draws profit from them. To all they give sustenance, to God glory, and to mankind consolation... May God grant that we, too, may have a share in this.[16]

Tauler concludes:

Since I am thus lost in the abyss
I no longer wish to speak, I am mute.
The Godhead clear has swallowed me into itself. I am displaced.
Therefore, the darkness delighted me greatly.[17]

Hadewijch: celebrate the capacity of your soul

The Beguine Hadewijch (d.1248) writes in similar vein in the 13th century. Sometimes the abyss is God's depth, and sometimes it represents the amazing inner capacity of the soul, a space for God to enter:

> Now understand the deepest essence of your soul, what 'soul' is. Soul is a being that can be beheld by God and by which again, God can be beheld… the soul is a bottomless abyss in which God suffices to himself; and his own self-sufficiency ever finds fruition to the full in this soul, as the soul, for its part, ever does in him. Soul is a way for the passage of God from his depths into his liberty; and God is a way for the passage of the soul into its liberty, that is, into his inmost depths, which cannot be touched except by the soul's abyss.[18]

Here is an echo of the Psalms' 'Deep calls to deep' (Psalm 42:7). In one of her poems she affirms: 'Where Love is with Love, in love / The abyss is unfathomable.' But immediately she goes on to say that this is no mere resting in Love:

> *There [in the Love of the abyss] all those who let themselves sink*
> *   in her*
> *Must be drowned in her;*
> *And to those who attend her in her nature*
> *She gives an unquiet life.*
> *Love springs out of her own nature*
> *And causes hearts, in Love, to be in constant striving…*
> *So it is allotted perturbation and turbulent unrest…*
> *Whoever loves must suffer many griefs…*
> *Oh, how deep is the abyss of Love,*
> *Which no one could know!*[19]

Angela of Foligno (1248–1309): fall into the double abyss

This Franciscan mystic has been called 'queen of the explorers of the beyond'.[20] Over the course of some two years, Angela enters into deep mystical experiences, often triggered by participation in the Eucharist and the sight of the Host and chalice.

First, she falls into the abyss of Christ's passion (her sixth step). A deep chasm envelops her, as she feels something of the physical and mental pains that Jesus underwent in the course of his crucifixion. She feels them both in her soul and in her body. She is overwhelmed at the *kenosis* of Christ, the distance he has descended from heaven to the depths of suffering. She feels she is participating in some way in his passion, his utter poverty, his sacrificial self-giving, his desolation on the cross.

There is an echo here of Francis of Assisi's prayer:

> My Lord Jesus Christ, two graces I beg of you before I die; the first is that in my lifetime I may feel, in my soul and in my body, as far as possible, that sorrow which you, sweet Jesus, endured in the hour of your most bitter passion; the second is that I may feel in my heart, as far as possible, that abundance of love with which you, Son of God, were inflamed, so as willingly to endure so great a passion for us sinners.

For Francis, this led to the experience of the stigmata, receiving the marks of Christ's passion on his very body. For Angela the experience is of being undone, dismantled, taken apart, an annihilation of the ego; she struggles with torments from demons, and all the ugly realities of her sins and vices confront her. A sense of self-knowledge is gained with fresh and alarming clarity, and her past is catching up with her. But intermingled with her anguish the overwhelming sense is one of unutterable thankfulness for Christ's suffering and passionate and compassionate love for humanity.

Then, there is a quantum leap into a further abyss—the depths of the love of the Holy Trinity. 'I truly heard these words,' she confessed after a mystical ecstasy, 'but it is in no way possible for me to know or tell of what I saw and understood, or of what he [God] showed me, although I would willingly reveal what I understood with the words that I heard, but it was an absolutely ineffable abyss.'

As if submitting to an unrelenting and irresistible gravitational pull, Angela allows herself to be drawn into the unfathomable abyss:

> I saw him in a darkness, and in a darkness precisely because the good that he is, is far too great to be conceived or understood. Indeed, anything conceivable or understandable does not attain this good or even come near it. My soul was then granted a most certain faith, a secure and most firm hope, a continual security about God which took away all my fear. In this good, which is seen in the darkness, I recollected myself totally. I was made so sure of God that in no way can I ever entertain any doubts about him or of my possession of him. Of this I have the utmost certitude. And in this most efficacious good seen in this darkness now resides my most firm hope, one in which I am totally recollected and secure.[21]

Now words fail her: there is nothing that can be said. She has reached the innermost recesses of her soul: 'There is in my soul a chamber in which no joy, sadness, or enjoyment from any virtue, or delight over anything that can be named, enters. This is where the All Good... resides.'[22] In the abyss of divine love, she can only swim.[23] Lachance sums it up:

> Pushed to the limits of the possible and the impossible, she felt more and more intensely the need to become empty, poor of every form of possession, to annihilate every image and representation, every word 'for words blaspheme'. In her journey into the obscure and yet dazzling darkness of God, she is drawn from within to go beyond the duality of heaven and

earth, good and evil, body and soul, and the divinity and the humanity of God to enter finally the space which is not a space, where the nothingness and the unknown abyss of self rejoin the unknown and ineffable nothingness of the divine life of the Trinity—a voluptuosity of suffering transformed into an infinite *jouissance*.[24]

Rowan Williams in his classic *The Wound of Knowledge* reminds us:

Illumination is the running-out of language and thought, the compulsion exercised by a reality drastically and totally beyond the reach of our conceptual apparatus... Real knowledge of God cannot be put into words with any approximation to completeness; thus real and personal knowledge of God cannot be identified with words in the understanding... God himself breaks and reshapes all religious language as he acts through vulnerability, failure and contradiction.[25]

Questions for reflection

1 How do you feel about the prospect of encountering God in the darkness of prayer? Name your fears, hesitations and hopes.
2 'To understand [the Christian faith] as a step into darkness requires a different frame of mind, a change of attitude for which we are little prepared.' How do you find yourself responding to Matthews' words? What changes do you need to make in order to enter the darkness of God?
3 Recall a time when you did find God, in some sense, in the dark. What lessons did you learn?
4 What is your default image of God—the one that you often come back to? Where did it come from? Do you feel ready and prepared to revise and change your image of God?

Prayer exercise

Centering prayer is a recent example of a way of praying in the West that encourages a deep realisation and experience of the God within. It suggests that by the inward recital of a single sacred word—like 'Abba' or 'Shalom'—one can come to a consciousness of the very presence of God within the soul. The word becomes a symbol of one's yearning for God or one's 'intentionality' in seeking to welcome a renewed sense of the indwelling God, and opens oneself up to the divine action within.[26] Prayer begins with using a word, but this prepares us for a deep, wordless, contemplative silence. Often the word itself can be left behind.

Either
Sit quietly in a relaxed position. Breathe in deeply and slowly. Choose a word that will get you started. Let this sink from head to heart. As Teresa says: 'The important thing is not to think much, but to love much.' Find yourself falling into the abyss. Do not try to hold on or cling on. Tumble, like Alice in Wonderland falling into the hole that opens up to her another world, underground. Stay below ground for as long as you wish. Then slowly make a return to the surface.

Or
This prayer time is in two phases. First, sit for a while in utter darkness. Let the darkness and silence speak to you of people's longing for God—their deep need for Christ's revelation. Also, as you quieten your heart and silence your lips, pray in the *apophatic* mode—with worldless wonder and no attempt at describing the divine. Second, when you are ready, light a candle before you. See how the light dispels the darkness. Look at the flame and find yourself praying that you will be a radiant light in the world, revealing the wonder and mystery of Jesus to others. Pray now in the *kataphatic* mode—affirming your love for Christ and attempting to find words to express your wonder. Pray that your light may intensify and burn ever brighter as you yourself discover more of him. Pray that epiphany may take place during your life today.

7

Facing the dragons: the dark side

Now the passage underground becomes treacherous. There are scary, slippery slopes, and clammy walls of rock seem to close in upon you claustrophobically. They are dark, damp, depressing. The air seems suffocating for a moment, the atmosphere teeth-chatteringly cold. A sense of dread threatens to grip and paralyse the soul: we are petrified! The subterranean world now becomes a forbidding, confusing and disorientating labyrinth. We sense a tremor in our soul: tension rises in us, as we try to suppress a feeling of alarm and agitation, but this might turn out to be but the prelude to a fresh experience of release and liberation. We are stumbling, scrambling, groping for a way forward in pitch blackness. In the murky depths, we suspect, demons lurk and dragons growl. Shadows loom menacingly. This is the underside, the nadir of the soul, the nether regions, our personal 'dark side'. God asks us:

> Have you… walked where the Abyss is deepest?
> Have you been shown the gates of Death
>   or met the janitors of Shadowland?
>
> JOB 38:16–17, JB

Dante depicted his descent into the Inferno of the underworld as an encounter with the sins of indulgence, violence and malice. In the *Divine Comedy* he passes through the gate of hell, which bears an inscription ending with the famous phrase *Lasciate ogne speranza, voi ch'intrate*, cheerfully translated as 'Abandon all hope, ye who enter here'. Karl Rahner writes of a subterranean darkness in each of us:

to which, although [it] may be part of us, we have no easy access, [a] depth in which demons may well lurk. It is full of mysterious psychic realities behind each of which stands something even more concealed and incomprehensible... There is within us a confusion of drives and possibilities...[1]

We are entering, literally, the place of trial and terror. The cave becomes a dungeon. Two places in Jerusalem summon the pilgrim down into depths that, at first at least, feel foreboding. Both are connected with the passion and incarceration of Christ.

On Mount Zion a dark cave is known as the Sacred Pit. The Church of St Peter Gallicantu—'St Peter of Cockcrow'—marks the traditional site of the house of Caiaphas. Several flights of steps lead down to Herodian caves cut deep in the rock. One is identified as the prison into which Jesus was thrown while waiting for Caiaphas to assemble his fellow accusers on the night of the passion. Deep and claustrophobic, it evokes the psalm's cry: 'Out of the depths I cry to you, O Lord. Lord, hear my voice!' (Psalm 130:1). Another psalm, which Christians recall here, conveys the desperation of this incarceration:

I am counted among those who go down to the Pit;
   I am like those who have no help,
like those forsaken among the dead...
like those whom you remember no more...
I am shut in so that I cannot escape;
   my eye grows dim through sorrow.
PSALM 88:4–5, 8–9

In Jerusalem pilgrims also visit the Prison of Christ, cared for by the Orthodox Church. Located on the Via Dolorosa, the Way of the Cross, this complex of deep dark caves is located near Pilate's Antonia Fortress and is identified as the place Christ was incarcerated by the Roman soldiers and subjected to abuse and degradation. The prison itself is a deep cave. Holes in the rock indicate where ropes or chains were attached as manacles for prisoners. Niches carved out of the rock suggest prison cells. The prison is a gloomy, unadorned space on several levels: as one descends towards the basement one plunges into the desolation of the story of the passion related in the Gospels. Above ground, a chapel of the Partorium recalls Jesus on trial before Pilate.

In the Bible, caves represent negative human experiences. First, caves are places of death; the first cave to be mentioned, the Cave of Machpelah in Hebron, is where Abraham seeks to lay his dead wife. They are tombs, graves, scenes of sadness and grief. In the Hebrew scriptures the cave often recalls the Pit of Sheol, the world of the dead, the underworld, the abyss. Josephus gloomily states: 'Hades is a subterranean place, wherein the light of this world does not shine… there must be in it perpetual darkness.'[2] The Pit represented death and fear, Psalm 30:9 (NIV) asking: 'What gain is there in my destruction, in my going down into the pit? Will the dust praise you? Will it proclaim your faithfulness?' John's Gospel tells us about a cave of death: at the tomb of Lazarus, 'Jesus wept' (John 11:35, RSV): 'Jesus, again greatly disturbed, came to the tomb. It was a cave, and a stone was lying against it.' But from the darkness springs hope: 'Jesus said, "Take away the stone… Did I not tell you that if you believed, you would see the glory of God?"' (John 11:38–40).

Second, caves in the Bible are places of refuge and fear, boltholes for retreat from danger. 'The hand of Midian prevailed over Israel; and because of Midian the Israelites provided for themselves hiding-places in the mountains, caves and strongholds' (Judges 6:2; see also Isaiah 2:21). Desperate lamentations and cries for help echo from the depths. Psalm 142, called 'A Maskil of David. When he was in the cave', links to his escape to the cave of Adullam (1 Samuel 22:1): 'With my voice I cry to the Lord… Bring me out of prison…' Psalm 57 is likewise attributed to 'David… when he fled from Saul, in the cave': 'in the shadow of thy wings I will take refuge, till the storms of destruction pass by' (Psalm 57:1, RSV).[3]

God enters the depths

The caves declare that God reaches down to the deepest human need. There is no dark corner, no recess of grief, no hidden fear, no gloom of bereavement, no abyss of despair, no emptiness, no depths of misery that God cannot enter and transform. The God of the New Testament is a descending God. As Paul celebrates in his letter to the Philippians (chapter 2), Jesus humbles himself and empties himself to be found in human form, so that even the underworld may bend the knee at the name of such a God.

At Bethlehem itself the focal point of devotion and pilgrimage is the Cave of the Nativity under Justinian's sixth-century basilica. The religious imagination, fed by images from Christmas cards or nativity plays, expects to find a wooden-roofed stable in Bethlehem; the pilgrim instead encounters a mysterious cave deep in the earth. As Justin Martyr wrote in AD160 in his *Dialogue with Trypho the Jew*, 'When the Child was born in Bethlehem, because there was nowhere to rest in that place, Joseph went into a cave very close to the village.' Origen, writing in 248 testifies: 'In Bethlehem you are shown the cave where he was born... Even those who do not share our faith recognize that the Jesus whom Christians adore was born in this cave.'[4] What is the significance of Jesus being born in a cave?

It is precisely *there, in the depths of human need*, that he begins his redeeming work. In the incarnation, the divine Creator Word enters the very depth of creation. The Orthodox liturgy notices the significance of the cave of Bethlehem, celebrating the paradox of the Maker of the heavens coming to be contained in the earth: 'Triumph O Zion... receive the Creator who is contained within a cave!'[5] A Compline hymn wonders at the divine condescension: 'When the creation beheld Thee born in a cave, who hast hung the whole earth in the void above the waters, it was seized with amazement and cried: "There is none holy save Thee, O Lord."'[6] It marvels at the *kenosis* or self-emptying in the descent of the divine Word:

Hearken O heaven, and give ear O earth.
Let the foundations be shaken, and let trembling lay hold upon the
nethermost parts of the world.
For our God and Creator has clothed himself in created flesh...
O the depth of the riches of the wisdom and knowledge of God![7]

Or as the Western antiphon for Christmas Eve puts it: 'For while all things were in quiet silence, and the night was in the midst of her course, Thy almighty Word leapt down from heaven from thy royal throne.'[8]

'The light shines in the darkness, and the darkness did not overcome it' (John 1:5). Divine light dispels human shadows: 'The people who walked in darkness have seen a great light; those who dwelt in a land of deep darkness, on them has light shined' (Isaiah 9:2, RSV). The central feature of the Orthodox icon of the nativity is the pitch-black hole in the centre of the design, the dark deep cavern in the earth into which the divine Word descends. The icon depicts the powerful beam of light from the heavens penetrating the deepest darkness in the radiant and life-giving birth of the Redeemer. But the icon of the nativity anticipates the passion: birth points to death. The child swaddled tightly in a band of cloth in a stone crib suggestive of a sarcophagus foreshadows the man wrapped in a death shroud in the tomb and points forward to his experience of being bound as a prisoner in the passion.

The liberator becomes the captive

There is a powerful statue of Jesus in Jerusalem at the Church of St Peter Gallicantu. Before beginning one's descent to the Sacred Pit, the pilgrim is confronted by a startling statue: Jesus is in chains, his hands tightly bound; the liberator becomes the captive, the prisoner. We realise afresh that Jesus does not come into the human situation as a miracle worker from outer space, as a drop-in problem solver or as a kind of emergency doctor sorting out a crisis and then nipping off; he comes to share the depths of our pain, he plunges himself into the reality of our suffering and stands in closest solidarity with those who suffer. 'He made captivity itself a captive' (Ephesians 4:8). He comes into our very midst and alongside us. In his passion, he places himself into the merciless hands of police and soldiers.

In our very midst Jesus suffers today and invites us to discern his features in the faces of those who suffer now. The theologian Paul Tillich makes central to his understanding of salvation the idea of God's participation in human pain:

> in the Cross of the Christ the divine participation in existential estrangement becomes manifest… God participates in the suffering of existential estrangement, but his suffering is not a substitute for the suffering of the creature… the suffering of God, universally and in the Christ, is the power which overcomes creaturely self-destruction by participation and transformation.[9]

Pascal wrote: 'Christ is in agony until the end of time.' In our very midst he falls and rises today. Today he finds himself in the dirt and dust, sharing the experience of those whose human rights are trampled upon. Today he bleeds as blades of rejection are thrust into human flesh in warfare or violence. Christ walked the Way of the Cross not solely as 'Jesus of Nazareth', as if he were one solitary, private, individual. Rather he walked this way as the new Adam, as everyman/everywoman, representing humanity itself. As Suffering Servant he embodied the destiny of a people (Isaiah 53). As Son of Man he becomes a corporate, inclusive figure, encompassing all, and he calls us to find him in the broken and the downtrodden, to recognise his very presence in those who are hurting (Matthew 25). We are invited to discern his features in the faces of those who suffer today in the world.

Release from inner prisons

In his dialogue with opponents and seekers in John 8, Jesus identifies and names captivities of mind and heart:

> Then Jesus said to the Jews [or Judeans] who had believed in him, 'If you continue in my word, you are truly my disciples; and you will know the truth, and the truth will make you free.' They answered him, 'We are descendants of Abraham and have never been slaves to anyone. What do you mean by saying, "You will be made free"?' Jesus answered them, 'Very truly, I tell you, everyone who commits sin is a slave to sin. The slave does not have a permanent place in the household; the son has a place there for ever. So if the Son makes you free, you will be free indeed.'
>
> JOHN 8:31–36

The Pharisees represent a defensive and predictable mindset that excludes the possibility that God might be able to act outside their narrow categories. Jesus says to them: 'You judge by human standards' (8:15; the RSV gives, in a literal translation, 'according to the flesh'). They cannot conceive of the possibility that the Son of Man will be lifted up (8:28). Their mindset chokes their attitudes and has become a sinful and negative captivity, tying up their minds.

Jesus the liberator comes to set us free from narrow and negative thinking. He comes to release us from false images of God and from damaging images of humanity and constricted views of human potential. He comes to unbind us from the bondages of guilt and shame and from the distortions wrought in our attitudes by the ego.

God works in the darkness

In his passion, Christ penetrates the lowest parts of the earth, the underworld. He enters the captivities of human fear and despair, the most profound anxieties of humanity.

The Apostles' Creed tells us: 'He descended into hell.' Jesus is buried in the depths of the earth, but in the mystery of Holy Saturday the work of redemption is being accomplished silently, secretly, in the darkness of the grave. Christ is busy in the underworld: 'Christ… was put to death in the flesh, but made alive in the spirit, in which also he went and made a proclamation to the spirits in prison' (1 Peter 3:18–19).

Matthew gives us this saying of Jesus: 'For just as Jonah was three days and three nights in the belly of the great fish, so will the Son of Man be three days and three nights in the heart of the earth' (12:40, ESV). An Orthodox hymn sings the liberating truth:

You descended to earth's depths,
And smashed the eternal bars
Which held the captives fast.[10]

In the Orthodox Canon for Holy Saturday the cave, the tomb, becomes a treasure house:

The blessed Tomb received the Creator as one who slept
And was revealed as the divine treasure-house of life,
For the salvation of us who now sing 'Blessed art Thou, O God our
Redeemer.'[11]

An Easter Day hymn exults: 'Today the Master despoiled Hades and raised them that from ages past were in fetters and held in grievous bondage.'[12] The prison of the cave-tomb becomes the starting point for humanity's journey to freedom.

The dark night of the soul

For John of the Cross the place of darkness, the 'dark night', becomes a place of transformation:

> O guiding night!
> O night more lovely than the dawn!
> O night that has united the Lover with his beloved,
> transforming the beloved in her Lover!

The 16th-century Spanish mystic gave three reasons for using this image to describe aspects of the spiritual journey:

> We can offer three reasons for calling this journey toward union with God a night. The first has to do with the point of departure, because individuals must deprive themselves of their appetites for worldly possessions. This denial and privation is like a night for all one's senses. The second reason refers to the means or the road along which a person travels to this union. Now this road is faith, and for the intellect faith is also like a dark night. The third reason pertains to the point of arrival, namely God. And God is also a dark night to the soul in this life... These nights pass through a soul, or better, the soul passes through them in order to reach union with God.[13]

First, says John, in the dark we cannot actually see. In the deeper reaches of prayer, the Christian needs to shut down his or her five senses because they hold one captive in a state of attachment to the material world and activate one's self-seeking appetites. Sometimes our senses get us stuck to material things, so there are times when we need to pray with our eyes closed—in the darkness.

Second, in the dark one cannot easily make out obstacles or turnings along the path, so one must move forward in trust. 'We walk by faith, not by sight' (2 Corinthians 5:7). In one's relationship with God, John teaches, one must take the risk of moving forward without knowing the precise route, venturing into the unknown, where visibility is nil. In prayer we must be prepared to venture into undiscovered, unfamiliar terrain, along pathways we have yet to tread.

Third, John says, the darkness speaks of God himself as Mystery. God is not something one can box in and neatly label; God is quite beyond humanity's best concepts and categories. However, 'the dark night of the soul' is not for John a negative experience, but rather a time of growth and healing. The night, for John, is a place of radical transformation. It represents a time when one allows God to do his work powerfully within, reshaping and redirecting the ego, and leading one into a greater surrender to him. The darkness can also represent the times we think we cannot pray, when we can't find the words, and when we don't feel anything towards God, perhaps when we are spiritually confused. John assures us that abiding in the darkness of God can be authentic prayer. In the darkness we can make the greatest discoveries of God. John's poems echo the ancient hymn of Easter praise, the *Exultet*: 'This is the night when Jesus Christ broke the chains of death and rose triumphant from the grave! The power of this night dispels all evil, washes guilt away, restores lost innocence, brings mourners joy!' The very darkness of prayer can become a place of resurrection.

Sometimes it is necessary to wait in the darkness of prayer. The darkness resonates with a process of radical dispossession that John of the Cross sees at the heart of prayer's movement from egocentricity to God-centredness, a process in which God seeks to reshape us and convert the ego. The renunciation of one's own confidences enables a total surrender to God: the pain to be faced is that of being stripped of our egotistical powers. Follent puts it:

> The abandonment of self-mastery and the taking on of a radical dependence on God will necessarily be accompanied by a sense of being undone or being annihilated, yet such an anxiety is quite ungrounded. In fact, the discovery that one can

no longer find one's guarantees in oneself may indeed be a sign that progress in the life with God is finally being achieved.[14]

Embracing the shadows

Depth psychology invites us to explore our 'shadows'. Jung wrote: 'Everyone carries a shadow, and the less it is embodied in the individual's conscious life, the blacker and denser it is.'[15] But shadows may not necessarily be entirely negative. Sure, they can represent those darker sides of our personality that we do not wish to show to the world, so we suppress them and alienate them from our day-to-day operations and consciousness: things like anger, a critical, judgemental spirit, fear, avarice, greediness, a controlling spirit, crude thoughts, an uncertain sexual orientation. These may be distasteful traits that we criticise harshly in others, as we project them on to other people, forgetting that they are part of our make-up too. But they could be 'golden shadows': undeveloped potential, underappreciated talents or dormant gifts, that we haven't been able to give space to in our life, because of time restraints or fear of failure. We may admire these things in others but deny them in ourselves, feeling we couldn't possibly have the capacity to achieve such things. We have got stuck on the idea that such accomplishments are impossible for ourselves.

Jesus' words suggest that we might embrace such shadows, and make friends with them:

> You have heard that it was said, 'You shall love your neighbour and hate your enemy.' But I say to you, Love your enemies and pray for those who persecute you, so that you may be children of your Father in heaven; for he makes his sun rise on the evil and on the good, and sends rain on the righteous and on the unrighteous. For if you love those who love you, what reward do you have? Do not even the tax-collectors do the same? And if you greet only your brothers and sisters, what more are you

doing than others? Do not even the Gentiles do the same?
MATTHEW 5:43–47

The 'enemy' may be within: that shadow aspect of our personality that we detest in ourselves. Jesus commends a proper self-respect when he commands: 'You shall love your neighbour as yourself' (Mark 12:31). We need to love ourselves and accept ourselves with the same kind of unconditional love that we see in Jesus as he embraces the prostitute, the tax collector, the 'thief' on the cross. We need to show to ourselves the kindness, gentleness, generosity and compassion that we would like to extend to others. Strategies are available that can help us embrace our shadow side.[16]

The tomb becomes the womb

The inner reaches of prayer demand radical, searing honesty. There is no place for pretence, for role-playing, for the wearing of masks before God. Here prayer gets real. Our self-protective barriers and defences must crumble before God. The false, competitive self must die. The self or ego identified with our persona (Greek: mask) that we present to the world must wither and fade away. The image of ourselves that we like others to see—confident, competent—is often shaped or conditioned by our culture, by advertisements, by the modern preoccupation with 'image' or cult of celebrity, by the compulsions and illusions of our age. People like a good performance. People want to see beautiful bodies, well dressed, unwrinkled, attractive. People admire the ones who seem to be wealthy and successful. They worship images of perfection. This is a self-image or image of the self that we would like to project on to others. We think that our worth, our value, comes from what other people say about us, how they acclaim us and appreciate us.

But as the Desert Fathers and Mothers found in the caves of the wilderness, this is the illusory self, clamouring for attention. It is a wax mask that must melt away. The Desert Fathers and Mothers went into the desert to discover God. In the process they discovered themselves too, including their dark side:

> One day when Abba John was sitting in front of the church, the brethren were consulting him about their thoughts. One of the old men who saw it became a prey to jealousy and said to him, 'John, your vessel is full of poison.' Abba John said to him, 'That is very true, abba; and you have said that when you only see the outside, but if you were able to see the inside, too, what would you say then?'[17]

In the depths of prayer, passions and lusts, fantasies and temptations are magnified and seen in all their ferocity as undermining our true identity in God. Anthony the Great said: 'there is only one conflict for him and that is with fornication.'[18] But he was also able to come to a fresh awareness of his true worth and identity in Christ. A striking feature of the *Letters of St Anthony* is his teaching about *gnosis*, self-knowledge. As Rubenson points out: 'Without knowledge of himself, or, as Anthony says, of his own *spiritual essence*, a man [sic] cannot know God, he cannot understand God's acts of salvation, but by fully understanding himself a man knows his time.'[19] Anthony's *Letters* celebrate a spiritual anthropology: 'A sensible man who has prepared himself to be freed at the coming of Jesus knows himself in his spiritual essence, for he who knows himself also knows the dispensations of his Creator, and what he does for his creatures.'[20] Fusing Platonic, Origenist and biblical ideas, Anthony teaches that humanity's 'spiritual essence' consists in being rational, that is, in our capacity for true knowledge of God. His advice is 'Know thyself.'

Thomas Merton observes that at the heart of what the Desert Fathers and Mothers are saying is the experience of the 'emergence of the true secret self':

> What the Fathers sought most of all was their own true self, in Christ. And in order to do this, they had to reject completely the false, formal self, fabricated under social compulsion in 'the

world.' A life of work and prayer enabled the old superficial self to be purged away and permitted the gradual emergence of the true, secret self in which the Believer and Christ were 'one spirit'.[21]

The cave of prayer becomes both a tomb and a womb: a place where the old illusory ego learns to die and where the new Self in Christ is born, a liminal place of undoing and remaking, of death and resurrection.[22]

Nouwen puts it:

> Solitude is not a private therapeutic place. Rather, it is the place of conversion, the place where the old self dies and the new self is born… Solitude is the place where Christ remodels us in his own image and frees us from the victimizing compulsions of the world. Solitude is the place of our salvation.[23]

Abba John realises that our true identity comes not from what other people might say about us, but from what God says about us: 'even if we are entirely despised in the eyes of men, let us rejoice that we are honoured in the sight of God.'[24] In the cave of prayer, in the experience of deepening enclosure by God, one knows deeply the affirming love of God. We have to return again and again to the deep reality of who we truly are in Christ. As Abba Isidore put it: 'in obeying the truth, man [sic] surpasses everything else, for he is the image and likeness of God.' Ultimately, this is the great discovery of the dark cave of prayer: a sense of who we really are in Christ. Initial fear of the underworld, then, passes into fresh confidence and hope.

Questions for reflection

1   What is your experience of 'the dark night of the soul'? In hindsight, can you discern any blessings or breakthroughs in it?

2 Name for yourself any 'dark shadows'—aspects or attitudes that you'd like to be kept hidden. What 'golden shadows' can you identify and befriend?

3 Why do you think it is significant that Jesus was born in a cave?

4 Have you found the time of prayer to be a womb or a tomb, in the sense the Desert Fathers and Mothers discovered?

5 Do you agree with Richard Rohr's affirmation: 'The path of descent is the path of transformation. Darkness, failure, relapse, death, and woundedness are our primary teachers, rather than ideas or doctrines.'[25]

Prayer exercise

When we name and face our 'demons' they cease to exert negative power over us: we have established a creative relationship with them. So reread the story in Mark 5:1–20, Matthew 8:28–34 or Luke 8:26–37. Allow it to speak to you symbolically and metaphorically of those patches of darkness in your own life that need healing.

He lived among the tombs
What things in your life are leading to death?

The chains he wrenched apart
What agitates you or disturbs you? What stresses you? What menaces you? What do you feel constraining or restricting in your life, holding you down? What is there in you that is desperate to get out, to find release or expression? It may be something negative, like anger; it could be something wholly positive, like unfulfilled creativity, unexpressed emotions, undeveloped talent. The 'demon' may turn out to be an angel!

He was always howling
What is your heart's cry right now?

[He was] bruising himself with stones
What causes your integrity or peace of mind hurt or harm? What damages your self- image?

He ran and bowed down before him
Turn your focus to the radiant and mysterious person of Christ.

My name is Legion; for we are many
What are the competing claims in your life? Do they pull you apart, pull you in different directions? Do you feel fragmented?

Send us into the swine
What repressed or suppressed elements in you need to be expressed, released? Breathe them out. Let go of them and pass them into God's hands.

So he gave them permission
Name the element that you want to pass into the hands of Jesus. Release your grip on it. Picture it running towards the mysterious deep. It does not have to drown! It can swim in the choppy waters, or it can fly!

Sitting at the feet of Jesus
Imagine yourself sitting at the feet of Jesus. Let the light of Jesus envelop the darkness and cast a radiance into your soul. Receive whatever he wants to give you. Take some deep breaths to inhale, as it were, his light deep into your shadows. Embrace the wholeness he wants to bring you. Realise you don't have to be perfect. Accept your limitations, but let them be bathed in the light of Christ. Know that you have a treasured, cherished place in the presence of Jesus: like Mary, who chose the better part and also sat at the feet of Jesus (Luke 10:39). Jesus has accepted you: accept yourself! Contrast the verbs in the early verses of Mark 5: binding, wrenching apart, breaking in pieces, crying out, bruising. Now the guy is *sitting*. Jesus has brought him to a place of stillness, resting in the new reality. Practise it. Let go of the bruising, cutting, wrenching. Let go, too, of the self-violence of

the blaming, the judging, the comparing. Learn to *sit*, still, at the feet of Jesus. Linger here as long as you can!

Clothed and in his right mind
The man's dividedness, represented by the 'Legion', split him apart. He is given a renewed mind. The divided, torn-apart mind has been clothed with 'the mind of Christ'. Now he is integrated, one, because Jesus has given him a new, unifying focus and mission. To this divided self, Jesus brings a radical reordering—a fresh centre of gravity, a refocused centredness, a new identity and a healing unity. As you wait in the silence, allow Jesus to clarify to you a renewed sense of purpose.

Go home to your friends
Allow Christ to give you, again, an overarching vision of what you are to be, a unifying vision. How would you sum up your essential vocation in one word? What is the overarching vision and purpose, uniting and integrating your life in your home and among your friends?

Tell them how much the Lord has done for you
Is there someone you can talk with about this? Now get up from sitting at the feet of Jesus: take some strides forward into the new future he has opened up for you in this liminal place!

8

Mining buried treasure: unearthing hidden gems

It is with a sense of excitement and expectation that we take in our hands, as it were, pickaxe and chisel: we are on a search, a quest. We have been told that there is treasure below: we may have to hunt for it, or it might confront us when we least expect it, like an unsuspected glint of gold in rock. We will need to be determined and utterly open to God's surprises. We will be fuelled not only by a sense of curiosity but also by a deep craving to know more of God, an unspeakable yearning for the divine. We must be ready for the unexpected, for the experience of awe and delight. What precious minerals or gemstones await us?

Many astonishing treasures have been discovered underground throughout the Holy Land. For Christians, the most exciting and significant is the excavation of the very Tomb of Christ, which had been deliberately concealed and covered over with earth in AD135 by Hadrian. He had constructed the platform of a small forum and a pagan temple over this site in order to stamp out early devotion to the place of the crucifixion and resurrection. At the Council of Nicea the bishop of Jerusalem, Macarius, asked the Emperor Constantine if the holy sites associated with the Gospel could be identified and properly marked. So they started digging. Eusebius of Caesarea, the fourth-century church historian, describes with great joy in his *Life of Constantine* how the cave of the resurrection was rediscovered in an amazing excavation beneath the earth in 326: 'as layer after layer of the subsoil came into view, the venerable and most holy memorial of the Saviour's resurrection, beyond all our hopes, came into view: the holy of holies, the Cave, was like our Saviour, restored to life.' A stunning basilica was built to preserve the findings, and the empty tomb has been a focus of Christian pilgrimage ever since.

Deep below the present basilica is a mysterious cave associated with the discovery of another treasure. Today, as pilgrims descend two flights of stone steps into the bowels of the earth, they pass stunning crosses etched in the rock by previous generations of pilgrims.

Finally, you arrive at a secret cavernous cave, in which a priceless treasure was discovered. Here in 326, it is believed, Queen Helena, mother of Constantine, discovered the True Cross—the wood that was used in the crucifixion. You find yourself standing in an ancient quarry, now deep underground; in the overhanging rock you see the chisel marks of the quarrymen. This relic is still venerated in the Church today, and the discovery has made its way into the Liturgy of Good Friday in the Western churches: 'Behold, the wood of the Cross, on which hung the Saviour of the World: Come let us worship!'

Other discoveries in the Holy Land astound and delight the pilgrim. The mysterious caves of Qumran, in marl canyons overlooking the Dead Sea, held for almost 2000 years the documents of the Essenes, rediscovered in 1947. These include an almost complete collection of Hebrew scriptures in Greek, and significant community documents which have greatly increased our understanding of the first century.

Israel is the most dug-up country in the world—and archaeologists are still unearthing priceless artefacts in the course of their excavations. Members of the Israel Caving Club discovered a large cache of ancient gold coins and jewellery in a cave in northern Israel's Galilee region in early 2015. The discovery was announced by the Israel Antiquities Authority (IAA) on 9 March 2015, and the exact location of the discovery is being kept a secret to preserve the integrity of the research area. Amateur spelunker Hen Zakai spotted a shiny object in a corner of a tight area. Two coins bearing the face of Alexander the Great on one side and a bust of Zeus on the other lay hidden behind a rock. The cavers alerted the IAA, who examined the items and recognised the find as 'something very, very unique'. Later, archaeologists uncovered silver earrings, necklaces, bracelets and rings in the cave, some dating to much earlier periods. Experts speculate that the items stashed in the cave were hidden during hard times and the owners intended to return to claim them. The cave is deep and has many more small crevices, which archaeologists hope will yield additional artifacts.[1]

Such findings alert us to the possibility of discovering great treasures in Christian spirituality. We recall the words of Jesus: 'The kingdom of heaven is like treasure hidden in a field, which someone found and hid; then in his joy he goes and sells all that he has and buys that field' (Matthew 13:44). The writer of the letter to the Colossians prays for his readers: 'I want their hearts to be encouraged and united in love, so that they may have all the riches of assured understanding and have the knowledge of God's mystery, that is, Christ himself, in whom are hidden all the treasures of wisdom and knowledge' (Colossians 2:2–3). Proverbs gives us a great promise:

> If you indeed cry out for insight,
>   and raise your voice for understanding;
> if you seek it like silver,
>   and search for it as for hidden treasures—
> then you will understand the fear of the Lord
>   and find the knowledge of God.
> PROVERBS 2:3–5

Job 28 celebrates the discovery of the most priceless treasure:

> Surely there is a mine for silver,
>   and a place for gold to be refined.
> Iron is taken out of the earth,
>   and copper is smelted from ore.
> Miners put an end to darkness,
>   and search out to the farthest bound
>   the ore in gloom and deep darkness.

They open shafts in a valley away from human habitation...
Its stones are the place of sapphires,
    and its dust contains gold...

They put their hand to the flinty rock,
    and overturn mountains by the roots.
They cut out channels in the rocks,
    and their eyes see every precious thing.
The sources of the rivers they probe;
    hidden things they bring to light.

But where shall wisdom be found?
    And where is the place of understanding?
Mortals do not know the way to it,
    and it is not found in the land of the living.
The deep says, 'It is not in me',
    and the sea says, 'It is not with me.'
It cannot be bought for gold,
    and silver cannot be weighed out as its price.
It cannot be valued in the gold of Ophir,
    in precious onyx or sapphire.
Gold and glass cannot equal it,
    nor can it be exchanged for jewels of fine gold.
No mention shall be made of coral or of crystal;
    the price of wisdom is above pearls.
The chrysolite of Ethiopia cannot compare with it,
    nor can it be valued in pure gold.

Where then does wisdom come from?
    And where is the place of understanding?
It is hidden from the eyes of all living,
    and concealed from the birds of the air...
God understands the way to it,
    and he knows its place...
And he said to humankind,
'Truly, the fear of the Lord, that is wisdom;
    and to depart from evil is understanding.'

The ecstasy of uncovering a hidden treasure is a deep, archetypal experience: we are invited here to discover something precious, of great value, perhaps long forgotten. Indeed, some of the treasures we will now take a look at have been long buried in the depths of the Christian tradition. This is because they were suspect, mysterious, not easily intelligible to rational orthodox minds which liked to imprison divine truth and mystery within dogma and doctrine. We will encounter sources that have been marginalised or even condemned by church authorities. Like evaluating semi-precious stones, people have not always appreciated their true worth.

Veritable treasure: our baptismal potentiality

Ephrem the Syrian poet, hymn writer and deacon of the fourth century (d. 373) tells us to approach the search with a loving desire:

Whenever I have meditated upon You
I have acquired a veritable treasure from You…
Your treasury seems empty to the person who rejects You.
Love is the treasurer
Of Your heavenly treasure store…[2]

The rich heritage of the Syriac spiritual tradition glints like specks of gold in the dark rock. St Ephrem represents an outstanding example. His great 'Hymn on Faith' shows us how he uses powerful imagery and metaphors in his description of the spiritual life:

See, Fire and Spirit are in the womb of her who bore You;
See, Fire and Spirit in are in the river in which You were baptized.
Fire and Spirit are in our baptismal font,
In the Bread and the Cup are Fire and Holy Spirit.

In this poem Ephrem celebrates the mysterious working of the Holy Spirit in the Eucharist and in the spiritual life. Echoing the story of the Syrophoenician woman (Mark 7) he writes,

*Look, Lord, my lap is now filled with the crumbs from Your table
there is no more room in the folds of my garment,
So hold back your gift as I worship before You,
Keep it in Your treasure house in readiness
to give it us on another occasion.*[3]

There certainly are many 'other occasions'—for Ephrem was a prolific and inspiring writer. He encourages us to see reality differently, using his famed image of the 'luminous eye' which can look into the hiddenness of God's mystery:

*Blessed is the person who has acquired a luminous eye
With which he will see how much the angels stand in awe of You,
     Lord,
And how audacious is man.*[4]

Ephrem encourages us to pray for the gift of the inner eye, which penetrates the deep things of God and gives true insight. In this way our prayer can become luminous, radiant and light-revealing:

*Let our prayer be a mirror, Lord, placed before Your face;
Then Your fair beauty will be imprinted on its luminous surface…*[5]

Ephrem represents one strand in the rich tapestry of the Oriental Orthodox churches. We might encounter too writings from the Armenian tradition, especially in the well-loved writers Gregory of Narek and Nerses Shnorhali.[6] For a modern restatement of Coptic spirituality, we might discover Matthew the Poor.[7]

Riches beyond imagining: Christ's self-emptying

The life experience of Jacopone da Todi (1230–1306) enabled him to encounter ever more deeply the love of Christ, and a favourite theme in his *Lauds*, poems of praise, is the discovery of riches and treasures.

His nickname means 'Crazy Jim' (he was baptised Jacopo)—he was an eccentric and passionate Franciscan friar in Umbria, head over heels in love with Christ. His discovery of Christ's riches came from adversity. He had been married, but his young wife died tragically. As a friar, he grappled with different versions of the Franciscan vision: the idealism and radical, real poverty of the 'Spirituals' deeply attracted him, and shone in a greater light than the compromised and more comfortable life of the 'Conventuals', who permitted the possession of buildings and were supported by Pope Boniface. The pope, enraged by Jacopone's harsh criticism of him, excommunicated him, and later he was thrown into the dank dungeon of an underground prison in a monastery in Todi. His stunning poetry exalts the love of Christ, and his descent from heaven to earth. Brother Ramon tells the story:

> The horror and fear that had caused him to shiver uncontrollably as he was forced down to his cell had now given way to a gentle passivity. It was not a passivity born of despair or resignation but rather a consequence of trust in the mercy of God… He had almost reached the point of accepting that the darkness of his cell was leading to his death. But at that moment of acceptance a new spark of hope was ignited in his heart, and burst into a gentle but powerful flame…

It was all part of the way, of the dark night of purgation. His prison cell had taught him detachment and abandonment to God and the beginnings of naked faith. He heard the words of Christ:

> *Soul, if you come to Me,*
> *Hear now then what I say:*
> *You can be Mine upon the Cross,*
> *There is no other way.*[8]

In the darkness of his subterranean incarceration, Jacopone discovered the treasure of Christ and the gift of a sense of amazement and wonder at the incarnation and the cross:

Wrapped in poor swaddling clothes,
You were utterly dependent…
Humble cloth which enfolded treasure
That puts to shame all gems and gold!

Christ says to him:

It is the love you have in your power that drives Me mad,
It is your heart I have always sought.
This is the prize I want to give you—
Myself and all my riches,
The treasure I brought with Me when I exchanged
The glorious life of Heaven for a cruel death…
I give you infinite riches you never dreamed of,
Your every desire will be satisfied…

Jacopone is overcome:

I sing for the birth of my Love;

He has redeemed me and slipped on my finger His ring;
I burn with love for Him who now appears in the flesh,
And embrace Him, He who is now my brother…
Lovers, come to our festive wedding:
Where Love is, there is joy.

He is one with us in loving riches and delights.
Soul, you are created anew—
Hurry to embrace your spouse
Who gathers you into His joy—O love, love!

He is intoxicated and energised by the love of Christ:

Love, jocund and joyous,
Divine fire, You do not stint
Of Your endlessly bountiful riches…

Generous Love,
Gracious Love,
Your riches are beyond imagining.[9]

Sparkling stones: our identity

John Ruusbroec (1293–1381) stumbled on a great discovery. He meditates on Christ's promise in Revelation 2:17: 'To the one who overcomes... I will give him a sparkling stone. On this stone a new name will be written, unknown to everyone except him who receives it.' For Ruusbroec, this gemstone is at once the treasure of Christ and our true identity in Christ:

> By this sparkling stone we mean our Lord Jesus Christ, for according to his divinity he is a beam of the eternal light, a ray of God's glory, and a spotless mirror in which all things have their life. Whoever overcomes and transcends all things is given this sparkling stone, through which he receives light, truth, and life.

He goes on:

> This, then, is the sparkling stone which is given to a contemplative; on it is written a new name, unknown to everyone except him who receives it. You should know that all spirits receive a name when they return to God—each a special name in accordance with the nobility of its service and the depth of its love. This name is different from that first name of innocence which we received at baptism and which is adorned with the merits of our Lord. Having lost that name of innocence through sin, if we still wish to follow God... then we will be baptized a second time in the Holy Spirit. It is then that we will receive a new name, which will remain with us for eternity.[10]

He explains further that the new name upon the sparkling stone represents each person's unique experience of God, our singular vocation to discover for ourselves God's touch:

> Whoever feels himself to be united with God savours this name… to the extent that each person can overcome himself and die to all things, to that same extent he will feel the Father's touch drawing him inward and will savour the sweetness of the Son's inborn fruit; by means of this savour the Holy Spirit will reveal to him that he is an heir of God. No one is exactly like anyone else as regards these three points, which is why everyone receives a special name, one which is continually being renewed through new grace and new works of virtue.[11]

Immortal diamond: our destiny and worth

As we recalled earlier, Teresa of Avila had stumbled on a great reality: the dignity and spaciousness of the soul. She had written in her *Interior Castle*:

> Consider our soul to be like a castle made entirely out of a diamond or of a very clear crystal, in which there are many rooms, just as in heaven there are many dwelling places… I don't find anything comparable to the magnificent beauty of a soul and its marvellous capacity… He Himself said that He created us in His own image and likeness.[12]

She is ecstatic in her excitement at this discovery: in the first room of self-knowledge, Teresa cries: 'O souls redeemed by the blood of Jesus Christ! Learn to understand yourselves!… The soul's capacity is much greater than we can realise.'[13]

Later she will ask:

> How can I explain the riches and treasures and delights found in the fifth dwelling places? Since in some way we can enjoy heaven on earth, be brave in begging the Lord to give us His grace in such a way that nothing will be lacking through our own fault; that He show us the way and strengthen the soul that it may dig until it finds this hidden treasure. The truth is that the treasure lies within our very selves.[14]

Teresa will go on to talk about other gems:

> Three things, especially, are left in [the soul] to a very sublime degree: knowledge of the grandeur of God, because the more we see of this grandeur the greater is our understanding; self-knowledge and humility… third, little esteem of earthly things save for those that can be used for the service of so great a God. These are the jewels the Spouse begins to give the betrothed, and their value is such that the soul will not want to lose them.[15]

Gerard Manley Hopkins, Jesuit priest (1844–89), stumbles on the treasure within: immortal diamond. In his poem 'Heraclitean Nature and the Comfort of the Resurrection', he imagines the whole of nature as did the Greek philosopher Heraclitus (c.500BC) as originating and ending with fire: 'Million-fueled, nature's bonfire burns on.' He realises that humanity is fragile and passing, vulnerable and contingent.

> *Man, how fast his firedint, his mark on mind, is gone!*
> *Both are in an unfathomable, all is in an enormous dark*
> *Drowned.*

But he wakes up to the difference that the resurrection of Christ can make:

> *Enough! The Resurrection,*
> *A heart's-clarion! Away grief's gasping, joyless days, dejection.*
> *Across my foundering deck shone*
> *A beacon, an eternal beam.*

Fresh confidence bubbles up inside him, as he glimpses the Christian hope:

> *Flesh fade, and mortal trash*
> *Fall to the residuary worm; world's wildfire, leave but ash:*
> *In a flash, at a trumpet crash,*
> *I am all at once what Christ is, since he was what I am, and*
> *This Jack, joke, poor potsherd, patch, matchwood, immortal*
> *diamond,*
> *Is immortal diamond.*

His descriptions of humanity as fragile clay or wood are juxtaposed with the glorious truth that we are destined to become the most beautiful and enduring diamond in God's sight through participating in the metamorphosis of the resurrection. We feel ourselves to be wounded, flawed, sinful, of little worth. We are actually, in Christ, beautiful, radiant and indestructible as diamond. Paul put it: 'in a moment, in the twinkling of an eye, at the last trumpet... we will be changed. For this perishable body must put on imperishability, and this mortal body must put on immortality' (1 Corinthians 15:52–53).

Thomas Merton writes of our inviolable dignity:

At the centre of our being is a point... which is untouched by sin and by illusion, a point of pure truth, a point or spark which belongs entirely to God... from which God disposes our lives, which is inaccessible to the fantasies of our own mind or the brutalities of our own will. This... is the pure glory of God in us. It is, so to speak, His name written in us... It is like a pure diamond, blazing with the invisible light of heaven. It is in everybody, and if we could see it we would see these billions of points of light coming together in the face and blaze of a sun that would make all the darkness and cruelty of life vanish completely.[16]

Richard Rohr contrasts the false self, marked by egotism and 'keeping up appearances', with the true self revealed to us by God:

> God uses everything to construct this hard and immortal diamond, our core of love… Diamonds, once soft black carbon, become beautiful and radiant white lightning under pressure. The true pattern, the big secret, has now been revealed and exposed 'like a treasure hidden in a field'… Diamonds are deeply hidden under miles, pounds, and pressure of earth and time, but like the True Self, like the thread, like the presence itself, they are there. And now YOU are there too.[17]

Below the surface, the façade, of superficial living lies the hidden treasure of our true worth. As we discover God in the depths, we discover our true selves too. We realise that we are, in God's sight, precious and valued beyond measure: we are loved for who we are and for what we are becoming. Diamonds, however, do not just appear—they are the result of a painful process of metamorphosis in which pressures and stresses and extreme heat play their part. Here below, we must allow God to shape and reshape us. But as John puts it, in time our true treasure will be clear: 'Beloved, we are God's children now; what we will be has not yet been revealed. What we do know is this: when he is revealed, we will be like him, for we will see him as he is' (1 John 3:2). John the Seer gives us this glimpse of the city of heaven:

> [He] showed me the holy city Jerusalem coming down out of heaven from God. It has the glory of God and a radiance like a very rare jewel, like jasper, clear as crystal… The wall is built of jasper, while the city is pure gold, clear as glass. The foundations of the wall of the city are adorned with every jewel; the first was jasper, the second sapphire, the third

agate, the fourth emerald, the fifth onyx, the sixth cornelian, the seventh chrysolite, the eighth beryl, the ninth topaz, the tenth chrysoprase, the eleventh jacinth, the twelfth amethyst. And the twelve gates are twelve pearls, each of the gates is a single pearl, and the street of the city is pure gold, transparent as glass.

REVELATION 21:10, 18–21

This is our destiny, O diamond!

The famous stone that turneth all to gold

George Herbert (1593–1633), the Anglican poet-priest of the 17th century, wrote that his poems were 'a picture of the many spiritual conflicts that have passed betwixt God and my soul'. His poems testify to an ongoing struggle to accept within himself God's unconditional love. Secular ambitions wrestled with a persistent and nagging sense of vocation to the priesthood, and Herbert finally gave in and was ordained deacon in 1626. But things were not to be straightforward for him. Illness and indecision delayed Herbert from entering full-time ministry and he was not ordained priest until 1630. Some of Herbert's most poignant and questioning poems were composed during these four 'wilderness' years. Herbert found himself appointed to a small and undistinguished parish church near Salisbury.

For just three years he was to exercise his ministry, until his death in 1633. He embraced the life of a parish priest with extraordinary devotion and dedication, and expressed his ideals for pastoral ministry in his work *The Country Parson*. But he faced different struggles during this period. Now he was no longer fighting against his vocation but, dogged with ill health, found himself questioning his usefulness. Though he valued the presence of Christ in the scriptures and in the sacraments, he wrestled with a sense of spiritual confusion and with the dilemma of unanswered prayer, and found himself echoing the sentiments of Jeremiah and the psalmists.

Then he stumbled upon a great treasure that would transform daily dreariness into a spiritual adventure:

Teach me, my God and King,
in all things thee to see,
and what I do in anything
to do it as for thee.

We have a choice. We can live life on the surface. Or we can see things more deeply, penetrate the dust:

A man that looks on glass,
on it may stay his eye;
or if he pleaseth, through it pass,
and then the heaven espy.

All may of thee partake;
nothing can be so mean,
which with this tincture, 'for thy sake',
will not grow bright and clean.

Herbert wakes up to a deeply sacramental view of life—a new way of seeing reality, glimpsing the presence of God in all things, which can be transformative.

A servant with this clause
makes drudgery divine:
who sweeps a room, as for thy laws,
makes that and the action fine.

Herbert has discovered the 'philosopher's stone'—an alchemy:

This is the famous stone
that turneth all to gold;
for that which God doth touch and own
cannot for less be told.

Herbert called this poem 'The Elixir'—referring to an extremely valuable stone sought by alchemists because they believed it had the power to transform common metals into precious ones.[18] This was the treasure he unearthed in a time of personal struggle to accept his true worth and potential in Christ.

Questions for reflection

1 What is the greatest discovery in your spiritual life that you have made so far?
2 Is there a way in which you can share this with others? Have you done so yet? What is stopping you?
3 Which of the treasures mentioned in this chapter most surprises you, astounds you, delights you? Veritable treasure: our baptismal potentiality; riches beyond imagining: Christ's self-emptying; sparkling stones: our true identity; immortal diamond: our destiny and worth; the famous stone 'that turneth all to gold'?

Prayer exercise: the greatest treasure of all

Teresa of Avila, in her *Interior Castle*, tells us that the ultimate treasure to be mined is not the Prayer of Quiet, or even the secrets of silence. It is the baptismal reality of the indwelling Christ. At the centre of the soul dwells Christ; this is an objective truth and nothing can take it away: 'in the centre and middle is the main dwelling place where the very secret exchanges between God and the soul take place.'[19] But paradoxically this place is set in the midst of the world's confusions and upheaval. As the Carthusian motto puts it: 'Stands the cross, still point of the turning world'.

Teresa is lost for words:

This centre of our soul... is something so difficult to explain...
That there are trials and sufferings and that at the same time

the soul is in peace is a difficult thing to explain… The King is in his palace and there are many wars in his kingdom and many painful things going on, but not on that account does he fail to be at his post. So here, even though in those other dwelling places there is much tumult and there are many poisonous creatures and the noise is heard, no one enters that centre dwelling place and makes the soul leave…

In our prayer exercise let us welcome the unshakable peace that the indwelling Christ gives, while remaining in solidarity with those who suffer.

Repeat to your soul, slowly, these words of Jesus: 'Abide in me as I abide in you' (John 15:4). Say these several times and let the reality sink deep within you: Christ is abiding, residing, at the centre of your being. *He* is, in fact, the very centre of the soul!

End by reading the words of St Paul:

Who will separate us from the love of Christ? Will hardship, or distress, or persecution, or famine, or nakedness, or peril, or sword?… No, in all these things we are more than conquerors through him who loved us. For I am convinced that neither death, nor life, nor angels, nor rulers, nor things present, nor things to come, nor powers, nor height, nor depth, nor anything else in all creation, will be able to separate us from the love of God in Christ Jesus our Lord.

ROMANS 8:35, 37–39

9

Calling from below:
subversive prophetic voices

Listen! Can you hear? From deep below us, we can catch the echo of cries, the sounds of strange voices that disturb us, shouts of protest. We feel a shudder in the earth, an unsettling vibration, a tremor. We recall that the word 'subversive', coming from the Latin subvertere, *literally means 'to turn from under, from below, from beneath'. The call of the prophets reverberates in our soul, calling us to courageous and decisive action. They give expression to the cries of the poor and refugee, the screams of the oppressed, the sobs of the broken-hearted, the sighs of the culture.*

Many caves in the Holy Land are associated with fugitives, rebels and prophets. At the foot of Mount Carmel, the cavernous cave of Elijah is a place of pilgrimage for Jews, Muslims and Christians. It recalls Elijah's prayer before his confrontation with the prophets of Baal, the threat of Jezebel's sword hanging over him (1 Kings 18). The cave of Elijah is a place to recall his encounter with God on Horeb. He had been fleeing many stressful situations, and finally enters a cave where he feels safe from his pursuers. A violent storm passes by. Elijah stands in the cleft of the rock: there he encounters God, and rediscovers himself.

> Now there was a great wind, so strong that it was splitting mountains and breaking rocks in pieces before the Lord, but the Lord was not in the wind; and after the wind an earthquake, but the Lord was not in the earthquake; and after the earthquake a fire, but the Lord was not in the fire. And after the fire a sound

of sheer silence. When Elijah heard it, he wrapped his face in his mantle and went out and stood at the entrance of the cave. Then there came a voice to him that said, 'What are you doing here, Elijah?'

1 KINGS 19:11–13

Reflecting on the experience of Elijah as related in 1 Kings 19, Dorothy Soelle (1929–2003) observes that Elijah did not linger in his cave, for the still small voice uttered a political charge: 'Then the Lord said to him, "Go, return on your way to the wilderness of Damascus; when you arrive, you shall anoint Hazael as king over Aram..."' (1 Kings 19:15). Soelle points out:

[After] the experience of God in the 'still, small voice' what happens now? Elijah does not withdraw into an act of worship; he does not make a pilgrimage to some shrine. Nor does he continue to divide things into the categories of sacred and profane, a division so dear to all religions. Instead, what happens is of significance for the Judeo-Christian tradition: the renewal of his political mission... he returns to the world.[1]

She is clear that prayer, if it involves a journey to a world within, must entail the remaking of the self—a re-energising—so as to enable the return journey to the outer world without delay.

Pilgrims also visit the cave of Elijah's successor, John the Baptist, located at Even Sapir near Ein Karem, his birthplace. This cave of 'St John in the Desert' celebrates the hidden years of John: 'The child grew and became strong in spirit, and he was in the wilderness until the day he appeared publicly to Israel' (Luke 1:80). It represents John waiting on God, his attentiveness to the divine. In this cave John clarifies his thinking and his mission: he begins to realise his vocation to be the precursor of the Messiah. In his desert cave, before John the Baptist spoke, first he had to listen. From childhood, John lingered in the desert. He was there for one primary reason: to discern and to clarify his essential message—listening to God, amid the rocks. When the time was right he issued his call to repentance. We usually read this in a moralistic way, calling us to penitence, but as recent writers have reminded us, 'Repent!' is a summons to an utterly different way of seeing reality. The word we translate as 'repentance' (*metanoia*) is literally, in the Greek, *meta* meaning 'beyond' or 'large', and *noia* which translates as 'mind'. John is calling us to 'go beyond the mind' or 'go into the big mind'. He is inviting us to a fresh way of seeing things, a new consciousness. He is demanding that we let go of our former narrow and defensive mindsets and make the transition into a new vision of things that Jesus sums up in the metaphor of the 'kingdom of God'. This cave tells us that before John speaks one such word, he first waits in the silence of listening and expectant prayer. The word of God springs from silence, from listening to him.

Jesus himself often passed caverns of fear. Towering over the valley path from Capernaum to Nazareth and overlooking the north-western corner of the Sea of Galilee near Magdala, the dramatic Arbel cliffs are honeycombed by 400 caves. In 37BC Galilean zealots barricaded themselves here, as Josephus tells us: 'lurking in caves... opening up onto mountain precipices that were inaccessible from any quarter, except by some tortuous and extremely narrow paths... the cliff in front of them dropped sheer down' (*War* 305, 310). The forces of Herod the Great reached the fugitive rebels by lowering cages down from the top: soldiers with flaming spears smoked them out to their death.

The Galilee of Jesus' time suffered the double trouble of oppression and poverty. Lee writes: 'Galileans... were oppressed, dehumanized and looked down upon. Galileans were marginalized by foreign invaders and also by the Jerusalem Temple-state...'[2] But above all, it was a place of deep poverty and need. The Galileans were crippled by heavy taxes: dues were owed to the Roman occupier, and temple taxes added to the burden. At the time of Jesus ordinary families were being forced to quit their ancestral landholdings, where they had lived for centuries, in order to meet these demands.

Land was also confiscated for the building projects and villas of the urban elite at Sefforis and Tiberias. But then they had to pay rent for what had been their own fields and homes: they became caught in a downwards economic spiral, becoming tenants in their own property. We should note how many of Jesus' parables speak of absentee landlords who impose severe dues on their tenants (see, for example, Luke 16:1–8; Matthew 25:14–30). Tax and rent robbed the Galilean peasant farmer of two thirds of the family income. Many were living at barely subsistence level. Greco-Roman culture nourished the creation of an upper class, the social elites, who owned great homes and estates. It was a world of 'haves' and 'have nots'.

It is against this background that we see, at the time of Jesus, the emergence of two significant expressions of resistance and protest against the status quo. First, there were the terrorists. 'Have you come out with swords and clubs to arrest me as though I were a bandit?' (Mark 14:48). The Greek word *lestes*, translated 'bandit', denotes freedom fighter or even terrorist. Josephus tells us about revolutionary activists based in Galilee who sought to undermine Roman domination by acts of sabotage or terrorism. Since the revolt of Judas the Galilean in 4BC the region had become a hotbed of Zealots' resistance to increasingly stifling imperial rule.[3] The hand-picked band of Jesus' disciples included Judas Iscariot; his surname may relate to the Sicarii rebels, forerunners of the Zealots. Also we meet 'Simon the Zealot' and the 'sons of thunder'. Maybe, therefore, a third of the Twelve were involved one way or another in the protest movement that was raising steam at the time of Jesus. Peter Walker writes: 'The Palestine in which Jesus grew up was… politically red-hot… The tension between the Jews and Roman rulers was increasing… Jesus [found himself] in a context that was like a tinderbox waiting to go up in flames.'[4]

Underground Church

The caves of prophets, fugitives and rebels remind us that not only did salvation spring from the depths of the earth, the Church too was an underground movement in more than one sense. Christians met and worshipped underground in the early centuries when facing persecution, in the catacombs of Rome and in underground cities of Cappadocia. The Church was an underground movement also in the sense that it was deeply countercultural, holding to values quite different from those of society; it understood its mission in terms of being a hidden but effective agent of God's work, like yeast and salt (Matthew 5:13). In Rome, from the second century a vast network of underground passages was excavated close to roads leading out of Rome (like the Appian Way), first of all as subterranean cemeteries and burial places. Often martyrs would be buried there. But these warrens of tunnels and chambers were also used from time to time as places of refuge during the brutal Roman persecutions, and as places of training for witness: there are spaces big enough to accommodate gatherings such as the 'catechumens' or those in training.

In Cappadocia, 36 underground cities were carved out of volcanic tufa and lava: the widest one is Kaymakli underground city, while the deepest is the Derinkuyu underground city at 85 metres deep. Pre-Christian in origin, they were used by the Christians as places of refuge from oppression and attack, also bases from which to evangelise. Kaymakli underground city consists of a hundred galleries on eight levels, while Derinkuyu has carved-out caves identified not only as kitchens, stables and domestic usages, but also as chapels, places of baptism, and missionary training areas. It was from here that a prophetic ministry emerged.

What is a prophet?

The prophets of old both spoke the word of God and also embodied or symbolised the word in a dramatic action. The burden of the Old

Testament prophets was not prediction of the future, but rather declaring God's word into the present situation, naming the idols and illusions of contemporary society. For example, Amos was concerned to deliver his people from self-satisfying rituals and self-absorbing forms of prayer, and alert them to the desperate needs of the society around them:

> I hate, I despise your festivals...
> But let justice roll down like waters,
>   And righteousness like an ever-flowing stream.
> AMOS 5:21, 24

In similar vein Isaiah is uncompromising:

> Is this not the fast that I choose:
>   to loosen the bonds of injustice,
>   to undo the thongs of the yoke,
> to let the oppressed go free...
> Is it not to share your bread with the hungry...?
> ISAIAH 58:6-7

Walter Brueggeman in his classic, *The Prophetic Imagination*, tells us that the role of the prophet is to envision an alternative consciousness, and to open up for people a different vision of things. The role of the prophet is to enable an alternative perspective which may be subversive, questioning, compassionate, and which certainly reveals itself in countercultural lifestyle and political choices.[5]

Subversive gospel

The gospel itself is subversive as it throws up radical questions about society and its status quo, undermining its cultural norms. Scholars point out that the one subject most likely to lead to conflict with the Roman authorities is the question of rule—and Jesus frames his message precisely around the concept of the reign of God: what would life look like if God, not Caesar, were on the throne?[6] Jesus' kingdom of God directly questioned the prevailing status quo of the kingdom of Rome. Indeed, Jesus challenges both the imperial powers and the conventions of first-century Judaism by his message about the divine kingdom, where all are welcome and all are equal. The kingdom of God represents a new way of living, a different path, an alternative vision for society, and the Sermon on the Mount reads like a radical manifesto. It all seems defiance. Jesus *is* a rebel in the eyes of Rome and crucifixion is the imperial reward for insurgents: the murderous insurrectionist Barabbas was released, while Jesus hung. In contrast to the brutal strategy of the guerrilla fighters and activists, crucified to left and right, Jesus becomes a rebel by peacefully advancing the reign of God. He, the non-violent one, is pinned to the cross, between the violent alternatives.

While the Gospels tell us that Jesus met his death as a rebel against Rome, they communicate the subversive ministry of Jesus through a closely linked image of Jesus the prophet. Those on Emmaus Road spoke of 'Jesus of Nazareth, who was a prophet mighty in deed and word before God and all the people' (Luke 24:19). In the synagogue at Nazareth, at the very start of his public ministry, Jesus chooses a text from the prophet Isaiah to be the manifesto for his ministry: he, too, is called 'to bring good news to the poor... to proclaim release to the captives' (Luke 4:17–21).

How does Jesus model for us a prophetic spirituality?

Provocative deeds. At the event sometimes called the 'cleansing of the temple', Jesus quotes Jeremiah and Isaiah and thereby locates himself in the tradition of Jerusalem prophets (Isaiah 56:7; Jeremiah 7:11). This event is best interpreted as a prophetic action declaring in word and deed the ending of the temple worship.

Pastoral encounters. Jesus models a prophetic lifestyle also in his pastoral encounters. At Nain, after Jesus has spoken words of hope to a grieving widow and lifted up her dead son to new life, the people 'glorified God, saying, "A great prophet has risen among us!"' (Luke 7:16). Jacob's Well witnesses the woman's acclamation: 'Sir, I see that you are a prophet' (John 4:19). In Jerusalem, he is hailed in prophetic terms: 'So they said again to the blind man, "What do you say about him? It was your eyes he opened." He said, "He is a prophet"' (John 9:17).

Political actions. Sometimes Jesus shows us a prophetic approach in his behaviour and proactive critique of Rome or Judaism. At the Palm Sunday entry into Jerusalem the crowds hailed him: 'This is the prophet Jesus from Nazareth in Galilee' (Matthew 21:11). Soon afterwards, we read, 'They wanted to arrest him, but they feared the crowds, because they regarded him as a prophet' (Matthew 21:46).

In the fourth Gospel, Jesus is twice acclaimed a prophet in a context about political choices. 'When the people saw the sign that he had done, they began to say, "This is indeed the prophet who is to come into the world"' (John 6:14). There was a division among the people: 'When they heard these words, some in the crowd said, "This is really the prophet"' (John 7:40).

Developing a prophetic spirituality: five challenges

1 Alternative lifestyle

Perhaps one of the greatest challenges facing us is that we have accommodated unthinkingly to the spirit of the age and our outward lives don't look very different from those of people around us. We are infected by the plague of individualism and the mindset of the consumer. Our households should model a lifestyle that questions the status quo of society. The hardest thing is to live simply.[7]

We need to learn the art of rebellion in relation to aspects of the culture that the gospel must critique. We need to learn to laugh at and scorn the advertising inflicted on us that tries to convince us of the need for a luxury item, where there is none. We need to show solidarity with the hurting and 'stand up and be counted' on issues that undermine the sanctity of life and inalienable human rights. But there are contentious or confusing issues where the Spirit may be speaking to us through God's world and not through synods. This happens sometimes! We have to read 'what the Spirit is saying to the churches' on issues like human sexuality: sometimes God might be calling out to us through the experience of those who have been alienated and despised.

In the face of materialistic, consumerist ways of living, the Church is challenged afresh to pioneer lifestyles that are different, alternative, in tune with the gospel, which indeed will go against the grain, against the flow, and be countercultural in this present age.[8] Postmodernism exposes the moral and spiritual vacuum at the heart of Western society. We must be alert to the emptiness of current hedonism and to a sense of spiritual bankruptcy which cries out for the experience of God revealed in a lifestyle marked by authenticity and simplicity. Dare to be different! John Dear puts it:

> Following Jesus today in a land of nuclear weapons, rampant racism, and widespread economic injustice means actively going against our culture of violence. As the culture promotes violence, we promote Jesus' nonviolence. As the culture calls for war, we call for Jesus' peace. As the culture supports racism, sexism, and classism, we demand Jesus' vision of equality, community and reconciliation. As the culture insists on vengeance and execution, we pray with Jesus for forgiveness and compassion. As the culture summons us to be successful, to make money, to have a career, to get to the top, and to be number one, we race in the opposite direction and go with Jesus into voluntary poverty, powerlessness, humility, suffering and death. Discipleship to Jesus, according to the Gospel, requires that we love our enemies, demand justice for the poor, seek liberation of the oppressed, visit the sick and the imprisoned...

create community, beat swords into ploughshares… If we try to engage in these social practices, we will feel the sting of discipleship and the Gospel will come alive.[9]

2 Prophetic struggle

An incarnational model of ministry demands that we get down below, in the gutter and in the dirt, where the poor and wounded are to be found. We will not be in ivory towers but find ourselves on ground zero, joining the struggle and standing shoulder to shoulder with the crushed and the little ones. We might take another look at the balance in our lives between action and contemplation, between struggle and silence. There is a 'a time to keep silence, and a time to speak' (Ecclesiastes 3:7). As Casaldaliga and Vigil put it:

We are called to live contemplation in liberative activity, decoding surroundings made up of grace and sin, light and shade, justice and injustice, peace and violence, discovering in this historical process the presence of the Wind that blows where it will… in the wail of a child, or in the full-throated cry of a people, we try to 'listen' to God…[10]

The Archbishop of Canterbury has spoken recently of the need for a 'revolution':

As Pope Francis has recalled so memorably, we are to be a poor church for the poor, however and wherever poverty is seen, materially or spiritually. That is a revolution. Being a poor church means… prophetic challenge in a country that is still able and has the resources to reduce inequality…[11]

Such a 'revolution' needs rebels who are prepared to speak prophetic words to those who have responsibility in our society.

3 Outspoken witness

Courageous priests and people from history and the present day inspire and hearten us. St Francis reveals the dilemmas of being a rebel. He was intensely loyal to the Church, submitting his Rules for papal approval and honouring priests because they bring to God's people the sacrament of love. However, he defied authority not so much by his words but by modelling a radically alternative lifestyle that called into question the hedonistic capitalism of his time: 'preach the Gospel always, and use words when necessary.'

4 Risky care

We are summoned to discover a scruffy and bleeding Christ in the broken and marginalised, and to honour him in them (Matthew 25:35–40). We should be angry and outraged at poverty, exploitation and social exclusion, while remaining ready to glimpse Christ in the wounded, and minister to him, without counting the cost:

> 'I was hungry and you gave me food, I was thirsty and you gave me something to drink, I was a stranger and you welcomed me, I was naked and you gave me clothing, I was sick and you took care of me, I was in prison and you visited me.' Then the righteous will answer him, 'Lord, when was it that we saw you hungry and gave you food, or thirsty and gave you something to drink? And when was it that we saw you a stranger and welcomed you, or naked and gave you clothing? And when was it that we saw you sick or in prison and visited you?' And the king will answer them, 'Truly I tell you, just as you did it to one of the least of these who are members of my family, you did it to me.'

A prophetic spirituality can be symbolised in hands and ears. Holy hands uplifted in prayer become hands outstretched in care, hands that may become dirty, bruised, wounded. We have, as it were, two ears: one to listen to God, one to listen to the cries of the poor, the screams of the exploited—which might turn out to be the cry of God himself.

5 Courageous prayer

There are big questions that we might ask about our own spirituality and prayer. Are there danger signs that my spirituality is becoming narcissistic, self-centred, closed in on itself? Is my spirituality about self-fulfilment or about empowering sacrificial living? If the measure of spiritual maturity is increasing solidarity with the hurting, an enlarging capacity for compassion, what are the signs that I am maturing? Is my heart getting bigger? How far can I allow the pain of the world to enter my prayer? Does my prayer have room for the oppressions and injustices of the world? What place is there for a costly intercession which is inseparable from self-offering (and does not let me 'off the hook')?

Indeed, what is my understanding of intercession? Is it advising the Almighty or 'coming before God with the people on your heart' (Michael Ramsey)? What place is there in my prayer for the cross— not only in terms of seeking personal forgiveness but in realising that God suffers among us? What does Matthew 25 look like in my experience? What is the evidence? Am I drawn to the margins in any way? As Jim Wallis puts it: 'Personal piety has become an end in itself instead of the energy for social justice... Prophetic spirituality will always fundamentally challenge the system at its roots and offer genuine alternatives based on values from our truest religious, cultural and political traditions.'[12]

'God's foolishness is wiser than human wisdom' (1 Corinthians 1:25). The early Church was a subversive community, for the apostles were described as 'people who have been turning the world upside down' (Acts 17:6). When the Church emerged, after the persecutions, into the Constantinian light of day, accommodations to culture and society were made. When Church and State fused in the Byzantine centuries, the Church forgot that her origins were from below, from the cave, her values discovered and forged in the darkness. We need to get down below and rediscover the caves of the prophets.

A radical discovery: amazement leads to resistance

Dorothy Soelle, whom we met earlier, is a prophetic voice in Western Christianity that challenges us, in the title of one of her major works, to make a link between *Mysticism and Resistance*.[13]

Teaching theology at Cologne University, in the aftermath of Auschwitz, she wrestled with the idea of an impassive, antiseptic God locked up in heaven, and came to see the God to be loved as suffering and present amid his people. Between 1977 and 1987 she taught at the Union Seminary, New York, where she was confronted by the imperative, arising from her life of prayer, to become involved in political action, leading her to speak out against the Vietnam War, the arms race of the Cold War and injustices in the developing world.

'Mystical sensibility' as she puts it—a capacity to encounter God and the fullness of reality—leads us to seek the divine not only in moments of spiritual retreat and solitude but in creation, in the mystery of human love, in the experience of suffering. She traces three movements in the spiritual journey as she offers a critique and rewriting of the 'Triple Way' sketched out in the tradition, which distinguished three successive stages of purgation, illumination and union. This enduring model of spiritual development had originated in the early centuries of the Church. Waaijman sums it up: First, people must repent so as to be freed from sin: this happens by a saving act of Christ (*via purgativa*). Second, they move into a stage where they learn to know the truths of the faith and the moral goals as Christ and the Church state them (*via illuminativa*). The ultimate stage focuses on the goal of complete sanctification by the Spirit who unites every Christian with God (*via unitiva*).[14] But in this view of the spiritual pilgrimage, there is an increasing introspection and removal from the world: it is a journey within.

Soelle, following Matthew Fox,[15] offers a fresh approach. First comes the experience of amazement at the mystery of God (*via positiva*). This dawning of wonder and praise starts to set us free from the captivities of our ego with its narrow self-centred thinking: 'the soul needs amazement, the repeated liberation from customs, viewpoints, and convictions, which, like layers of fat that make us untouchable and insensitive, accumulate around us.'[16] A second stage is characterised by a letting go of false desires and false needs, such as are fostered in us by consumerism. This may entail a 'dark night of the soul', a *via negativa*, as we start to part with the normal seductive attachments and the obsessions of our culture. God starts to work a transformation in our outlook and priorities, as we move into a third stage, the *via transformativa*. Here, two themes of healing and resistance are inseparable: as God leads us into a costly compassion for those who suffer, so we find ourselves standing up to expressions of injustice in the world. As Soelle puts it: 'every way of union is one that continues onward and radiates outward. Being-at-one is not individualistic self-realization but moves beyond that to change death-orientated reality. Being-at-one shares itself and realizes itself in the ways of resistance.'[17] She is emphatic:

> For me, mysticism and transformation are indissolubly interconnected. Without economic and ecological justice (known as ecojustice) and without God's preferential love for the poor and for this planet, the love for God and the longing for oneness seem to me to be an atomistic illusion... A genuine mystical journey has a much larger goal...[18]

She wrestles with the interplay between inwardness and involvement:

> The goal is to reconcile the two worlds... It seems almost impossible to reconcile the two: the magnitude of the inward

journey which we need for experience of self, and the way back into the society of a world that can once more be lived in. Inwardness and involvement are not companion attributes in most people, for sensitive people are often not communally inclined, and people who like to be communally involved are sometimes lacking in sensitivity. Prayer and work, labour and contemplation appear to be compartmentalized into two worlds... The critical question with respect to the expression of the deepest human experiences, those we regard as 'the inward journey', is the question of connection to and with society... Living as Christ lived means the inward journey to the emptying and surrendering of the ego and the return journey to the midst of this world.[19]

We find in the journey within not only an encounter with God but a clarification of our own identity in God, our destiny, and our vocation in the world. It is to this orientation that we must now turn in our closing chapter.

Questions for reflection

1   What would your life look like if you modelled it on Jesus the prophet?
2   When was the last time you were outraged or indignant about an injustice, near or far, and actually did something about it?
3   The ministry of the prophet is characterised by courage and audacity, by plain speaking and bold actions. How do these reveal themselves in your life?
4   Dare you be disruptive in relation to society's status quo? Do you play it safe and stay out of trouble? Is your life predictable or tame? Do you need to recover nerve and verve?
5   What would a prophetic spirituality look like in your context?

Prayer exercise

Use your hands expressively in this prayer time in four actions.

Begin by clenching your fists tight and holding them before you. Feel the tension and let these fists represent an anger or frustration that bothers you today, a situation in the world that you feel strongly about. Hold them before God in the solidarity of prayer and intercession.

Next, slowly open your downturned palms and let go of the tension. Let it fall away from you to God. In this gesture give to God any negative feelings or stresses; feel them drip out of your fingertips, as it were. Surrender the situation to God's providence and sovereignty.

Third, turn your hands upwards in a gesture of surrender to God and of receiving from God. Breathe in what God wants to give you right now—perhaps a reassurance that all will be well. Breathe in his empowering Spirit who will give you the courage for actiqn.

Finally, take a look at your hands. Is there an action that God is calling you to make in relation to your initial concern? What should you do as a result of this—something bold, something risky or rebellious?

Recall 2 Timothy 1:7: 'God did not give us a spirit of cowardice, but rather a spirit of power and of love and of self-discipline.' End with the Serenity Prayer: 'God grant me the serenity to accept the things I cannot change; courage to change the things I can; and wisdom to know the difference.'

10

Treading lightly— and moving forwards

We have been examining the ground beneath our feet and now it is time to return to the surface. Our eyes are blinking painfully as we leave the darkness below and face the dazzling sunlight. We are adjusting to the challenges of the environment in more than one sense. For now, it is time to open our eyes to the realities around us on the surface. We see a stunningly beautiful world and at the same time disturbing signs of the degradation and exploitation of the planet. As the parable of the sower reminds us, Jesus was alert to the state of the surface of the earth as he walked the hills of Galilee. He saw broken rocky ground with pitiable thin soils, and neglected overgrown fields choked by thorns and brambles. Looking at creation he gave this command and imperative, 'Strive above all things for God's reign and for his justice!'[1] It is time for us to take seriously the materiality of spirituality and the needs of the poor.

One of the most stunning underground experiences possible in the Holy Land is usually missed by today's pilgrim or tourist, even though it is very close at hand. The entrance to Zedekiah's Cave is just beneath the northern part of Jerusalem's Old City wall: there is an access point between the Damascus and Herod gates. Inside, a downward-sloping path leads into a vast cavern, 300 feet long. From the entrance to the furthest point, the huge cave extends about 650 feet. Its maximum width is about 330 feet and its depth is generally about 30 feet below the street level of the Muslim Quarter, although there are several lower levels and blocked tunnels too. The extent is over five acres. The walls of the awesome galleries still bear the chisel marks of the stonecutters. It is the largest man-made cave in the Holy Land and gives us an example of reverent mining and respectful use of resources underground. Although it is popularly called 'Solomon's Quarries' the rock cut away and mined here was utilised in the second, not first temple, when Herod the Great reconstructed it just before the birth of Christ. You can see huge, nearly finished building blocks still left in position, ready to be loosened carefully from the rock walls. Indeed, the massive blocks of stone kissed today in the Western (Wailing) Wall by Jewish pilgrims were mined from here. So the white limestone *meleke* rock—meaning 'royal' stone—was used for a sacred purpose and indeed is reverenced today. It is possible to extract materials from the underground in a thoughtful, not exploitative way.

As one descends many steps into the cave, past a vast, high-vaulted cavern, the size of a football pitch, an auditorium-like chamber, one hears a faint and mysterious sound. You are captivated by the intriguing sound of water. The gentle noise from a spring beckons you, allures you to go further down, further, deeper beneath the city. Finally, at the far end you encounter a trickling spring, and by it see a sign: 'Here flow Zedekiah's tears.' King Zedekiah had been the last Judean king in the sixth century BC; the tradition is that he fled here before being captured and blinded by the invading Babylonian King Nebuchadnezzar. Here, it is said, Zedekiah shed tears over the wanton destruction of the city and the dismantling and ransacking of the Jewish temple (2 Kings 25; Jeremiah 34). So this cave becomes a paradoxical place: it testifies to sacred, reverent use of the rock and also to wanton violence against the city.

Sadly, not far away are reminders of the contemporary abuse of sacred land. Today, plastic rubbish overflows bins and blows in the wind. There is very little recycling in the Holy Land. Solid-waste disposal in the land causes significant and irreversible damage to groundwater, air, soil and quality of life. In 2000, then-Israeli Environmental Minister Dalia Itzik stated that she regarded garbage disposal as Israel's number-one environmental problem. More than

95 per cent of the country's solid waste is buried in landfills, burned in open-air pits or left to rot in garbage dumps. The soil beneath our feet is often polluted and contaminated.

In addition, the sacred land has become a scarred land. Massive degradation and destruction of the environment has been caused by industrial-scale tunnelling projects, most recently for a new high-speed rail link between Jerusalem and Tel Aviv. The awesome Judean hills in the Occupied Territories are riddled with tunnels for settler-only roads, while a road network to bypass Bethlehem (now hemmed in by the 30 feet high concrete wall called the Separation Barrier) required a series of tunnels to be blasted by explosives in the ancient rock. Ancient olive trees are uprooted mercilessly every day. There are more ominous construction projects underground. Just ten miles to the east of Jerusalem near the Sorrek Valley—the most probable route of the road to Emmaus—underground bunkers and an extensive network of secret tunnels and emplacements hollowed out of the limestone conceal a hoard of nuclear-tipped long-range missiles. To the south of the country, amid the beautiful landscape of the Negev desert, lies Dimona's infamous nuclear research centre. All this alerts the pilgrim to the need to reconnect spirituality and physicality. We need exploration, not exploitation; respect and reverence for God's earth, not its rape.

While this book has adapted a metaphorical reading of the landscape, we must acknowledge that Christians have a problem of spiritualising the physical. This tendency has been present since the beginning. In his version of the Lord's Prayer, Luke turns Matthew's 'Release us from our debts'—a physical petition arising from a situation of dire poverty—into the more internalised 'Forgive us our sins'. In the Beatitudes, Matthew spiritualises Luke's raw 'Blessed are you poor' into 'Blessed are the poor in spirit'. It is often easier to conceive of spiritual things instead of getting our hands dirty. We forget that the root meaning of the very word 'ministry', *diakonia*, means 'through the dust'.

The problem of spirituality divorced from earthiness

So, as incarnational spirituality celebrates not only God within, but God in our very midst, in the dirt and in the gutter, the prayer of contemplation must of necessity lead to courageous and compassionate action. Prayer might begin with a sense of God beyond: 'Our Father who art in heaven'. But it dares to pray 'thy Kingdom come' and moves to an awareness of the God nearby: 'Thy will be done on earth as it is in heaven.'

Christian spirituality became infected with divisive, dualistic thinking as the Church in the early centuries embraced Platonic thought. Plato himself wrote in the *Republic* that attentiveness to the world of the senses was 'looking in the wrong direction'.[2] The key to life was to become radically detached from the concerns of the body. Origen (c.185–c.254) outlined a progress of successive stages by which the soul is invited to advance towards God. We see here the genesis of the Triple Way which was to be so influential in the history of Christian spirituality: a sketch of the spiritual life that moves from purgation or separation from the world, to illumination, to union with God. This is profoundly shaped by Origen's Platonic anthropology: the goal in view is for the soul (*psyche*) to become free from the attentions of the body in order to contemplate God as *nous*, mind. Evagrius (346–99) likewise taught that greater detachment enables greater attentiveness to God, a movement from the material to the immaterial.

So disastrous polarities crept into Christian thinking, undermining the idea of God's incarnation. Things were pitched against one another: heaven was opposed to earth, the body to the spirit. Politics and prayer were to be kept separate. Sacred and secular were delineated with barriers, as if they were two separate realms, holy and unholy. The Church and the world are set against each other. In spirituality, such dualistic thinking has created unnecessary distances chasms. When God is thought of as 'up there', prayer becomes detached from life. In works like *The Cloud of Unknowing* we encounter such advice as:

Do not occupy yourself either in your thoughts or your desires with any of God's creatures, or anything associated with them either in a general or particular way. One might think such occupation correct. But I tell you: free yourself interiorly from all creatures, and pay no heed to them... let the clouds of forgetfulness spread over them.[3]

A problem with definition

What *is* spirituality? 'It appears that spirituality is one of those subjects whose meaning everyone claims to know until they have to define it.'[4] As Professor Sheldrake cautions, spirituality has become a slippery and elusive word to define. In recent years, the word has been utilised in ever-wider contexts, far beyond the confines of church or even religion: indeed, the rise in the use of 'spirituality' to denote some kind of personal experience of awareness seems proportionate to the decline of the institutional Church.[5] A national study of college students' search for meaning and purpose typifies current usage of the term: 'Spirituality... captures those aspects of our experience that are not easy to define or talk about, such as inspiration, creativity, the mysterious, the sacred, and the mystical. Within this very broad perspective, we believe spirituality is a universal impulse and reality.'[6]

Does spirituality allude only to some ephemeral, elusive dimension of human existence? What can we learn from the history of the term? The word 'spirituality' translates the Latin *spiritualitas*, corresponding to Paul's use of *pneumatikos*. In his theology, Paul expresses the believer's new life in Christ as 'life in the Spirit' *kata pneuma*, 'according to the Spirit', contrasted with life outside Christ which is *kata sarx*, 'according to the flesh' (here 'flesh' denotes not body or physicality but 'life not ruled by God').[7] For Paul, 'all who are led by the Spirit of God are children of God' (Romans 8:14). The earliest recorded use of *spiritualitas*, in a text once attributed to Jerome, conveys this same sense: 'So act as to advance in spirituality.' It was only in the twelfth century that *spiritualitas* began to be used in contrast to *corporalitas* (bodily existence) or *materialis* (matter). In France in the 17th century the word 'spirituality' began to be used more widely of the spiritual life, referring to practices of prayer or devotion; ultimately it entered the English language in this sense of a 'means towards Christian perfection' in the early 20th century through the translation of Pierre Pourrat's *La spiritualité chrétienne*.[8]

In recent years Christian scholars have pointed to the transformational or transformative character of spirituality. Sandra Schneiders writes that 'spirituality as an academic discipline studies the transformative Christian experience as such'; while McGinn goes further and calls mysticism 'a process of personal transformation'.[9] Waaijman considers spirituality as a process of transformation taking place within the divine–human relationship.[10]

A definition of spirituality that entails divine–human encounter is offered by former Anglican Officer for Evangelism Robert Warren: 'By *spirituality* is meant our understanding and experience of how encounter with God takes place and how such an encounter is sustained.'[11] But such a definition does not go far enough, for it stops short of suggesting that such encounter changes people, makes a measurable difference to their lives. The late Methodist scholar Gordon Wakefield stresses this: 'Spirituality concerns the way in which prayer influences conduct, our behaviour and manner of life, our attitudes to other people... Spirituality is the combination of living and praying.'[12] Or as Dyckman and Carroll suggest: 'Spirituality is the style of a person's response to Christ before the challenge of everyday life, in a given historical and cultural environment.'[13] Leech puts it like this:

> I believe that we can speak of spirituality as a necessary bedrock and foundation of our lives, provided that we understand that we are speaking of the foundation and not of a compartment. To speak of spirituality in this sense is to speak of the whole life of the human person and human community in their relationship with the divine.[14]

Our spirituality must not become individualistic, fostering a 'personal relationship with God' at the expense of an incarnate spirituality grounded and earthed in the needs of the age: we must stay aware of the danger of what Hughes calls 'split spirituality'—piety which has become adrift from life.[15] Robert McAfee Brown subtitled his book *Spirituality and Liberation* with the words: 'overcoming the great fallacy'.[16] He identifies this as a persistent dualism that separates and opposes faith and ethics, the holy and the profane, the otherworldly and this-worldly—eroding the central Christian belief in the Word made flesh. Privatised spirituality is a contradiction in terms.

The Hebrew scriptures rejoice in creation

The poem or hymn of creation found in the opening lines of Genesis celebrates the goodness of God's world: 'The earth brought forth vegetation: plants yielding seed of every kind, and trees of every kind bearing fruit with the seed in it. And God saw that it was good' (Genesis 1:12). The psalmist cries out:

> For the Lord is a great God,
>   and a great King above all gods.
> In his hand are the depths of the earth...
> **PSALM 95:3–4**

At the centre of the Bible the rich poem of the Song of Songs invites us to enjoy a spontaneous delight in the beauty of creation and to rediscover a sacramental approach to the world.[17] In this Wisdom literature, the garden becomes a meeting place for lovers, place of the tryst, the bride and groom celebrating their love. It resonates with a key life-affirming undercurrent in Jewish spirituality: the goodness and givenness of creation. Indeed, the most typical form of Jewish prayer is the *berakhah*, the blessing of God for his gifts: 'Blessed are you, Lord God, King of the universe...'

The Jewish prophets, alert to the earth

The Hebrew prophets, seeing the land as sacred, employ metaphors facing them each day in their very environment:

> I will be like the dew to Israel;
>> he shall blossom like the lily,
>> he shall strike root like the forests of Lebanon.
> His shoots shall spread out;
>> his beauty shall be like the olive tree,
>> and his fragrance like that of Lebanon.
> They shall again live beneath my shadow,
>> they shall flourish as a garden;
> they shall blossom like the vine,
>> their fragrance shall be like the wine of Lebanon.
>
> HOSEA 14:5–7

Jesus takes a contemplative look at the world

Summoning us into the new creation, Jesus invites us: 'Consider the lilies, how they grow' (Luke 12:27). 'Consider': the Greek word means 'turn your attention to this, notice what is happening, take a long, slow look'. Jesus summons us to a contemplative way of living, a deeply reflective way of seeing the world. Learn to perceive things differently. This sacramental way of viewing reality becomes a dominant theme in the fourth Gospel. Jesus sees wine, vines, water, bread, sunlight and candlelight, even shepherding, as speaking of himself. The other Gospels combine to give us the clear impression that this was an outlook on the world that was truly characteristic of Jesus himself. The secrets of the kingdom reveal themselves through the elements of earth, sky and sea: all creation becomes a parable of God's reign.

Christian spiritual writers

The sacramentality of creation is celebrated throughout Christian spirituality: in their commentaries on the Song of Songs, writers such as Gregory of Nyssa, Bernard of Clairvaux and even the Puritan John Owen observe how physicality and materiality point to spirituality: the love of bride and bridegroom speaks of Christ's love for his Church.

Gerard Manley Hopkins puts it:

The world is charged with the grandeur of God.
It will flame out, like shining from shook foil.[18]

William Blake in his poem 'Auguries of Innocence' invites us

To see a world in a grain of sand
And a heaven in a wild flower,
Hold infinity in the palm of your hand,
And eternity in an hour.[19]

One of the key concepts in the writings of Hildegard of Bingen (1098–1179), poet, mystic and musician, is 'greening' or *viriditas*. Today we talk about the greening of the planet, but 900 years ago Hildegard celebrated the presence of the Holy Spirit in the created order through the idea of greening: 'the earthly expression of the celestial sunlight; greenness is the condition in which earthly beings experience a fulfilment which is both physical and divine; greenness is the blithe overcoming of the dualism between earthly and heavenly.'[20] For Hildegard, the wetness or moisture of the planet, revealed in verdant growth, bespeaks the Holy Spirit who 'poured out this green freshness of life into the hearts of men and women so that they may bear good fruit'.[21]

She invites us to see the world differently: she even overcomes the dichotomy of heaven and earth by glimpsing the heavenly action in the freshness of the planet, which mirrors the human soul.

In the next century, Francis of Assisi displayed a remarkable kinship and sense of unity with creation. At the dawn of capitalism and a creeping consumerist approach to things—Francis was the son of a wealthy cloth-merchant and worked in his shop—he discovered a deep connectedness to all things which was honouring and non-exploitative. In his 'Canticle of Creation', he hailed the sun as brother and the moon as sister; he greeted Sister Water and Brother Wind, and in his ministry he approached the fearsome wolf of Gubbio as 'brother'. Franciscan prayer nurtures such an appreciative and respective approach to the world of nature, and overcomes what Martin Buber last century characterised as an 'I-It' relationship, nudging us towards an 'I-Thou 'relationship. The former regards the Other as an object to be studied or utilised for our benefit: the latter sees the Other as a subject in his or her own right who might just change us in the course of genuine encounter.[22] Francis invites us, indeed, to move from an 'I-Thou' relationship which still distinguishes and separates, towards a communion with the Other, symbolised in his embrace of the despised leper.[23] He invites us to recognise and celebrate the radical and essential interconnectedness of all things and of all people.

Contemporary approaches

Pope Francis opens his 2015 encyclical *Care of Our Common Home* with the words *Laudato Si'*—'Praise be to you, my Lord'—quoting St Francis' 'Canticle of Creation'. It is a passionate appeal to all people of goodwill to address the devastating effects of climate change on people and the planet. Pope Francis' encyclical emphasises the connection between environmental degradation and poverty, between the love for creation and poverty reduction, and the interconnection between human dignity, human development and human ecology. Peoples across the world are being pushed deeper into poverty due to the changing climate, and our faith moves us to speak out in solidarity.

In his chapter 'Ecological Education and Spirituality' Francis calls us to an ecological spirituality grounded in the convictions of our faith. Calling us towards a new lifestyle, he says that what we need is an 'ecological conversion', whereby the effects of our encounter with Jesus Christ become evident in our relationship with the world around us. Living our vocation to be protectors of God's handiwork is essential to a life of virtue; it is not an optional or a secondary aspect of our Christian experience:

> Christian spirituality proposes an alternative understanding of the quality of life, and encourages a prophetic and contemplative lifestyle, one capable of deep enjoyment free of the obsession with consumption. We need to take up an ancient lesson, found in different religious traditions and also in the Bible. It is the conviction that 'less is more'. A constant flood of new consumer goods can baffle the heart and prevent us from cherishing each thing and each moment. To be serenely present to each reality, however small it may be, opens us to much greater horizons of understanding and personal fulfilment. Christian spirituality proposes a growth marked by moderation and the capacity to be happy with little. It is a return to that simplicity which allows us to stop and appreciate the small things, to be grateful for the opportunities which life affords us, to be spiritually detached from what we possess, and not to succumb to sadness for what we lack. This implies avoiding the dynamic of dominion and the mere accumulation of pleasures.[24]

We are being summoned from a pragmatic and self-centred consumer mentality, so deeply entrenched in our culture and mindset, to seeing creation as not an entity to be manipulated or exploited but a divine presence to be honoured.[25] We join with Francis in his prayer:

> God of love, show us our place in this world
> as channels of your love for all the creatures of this earth,

for not one of them is forgotten in your sight.
Enlighten those who possess power and money
that they may avoid the sin of indifference,
that they may love the common good,
advance the weak, and care for this world in which we live.
The poor and the earth are crying out.
O Lord, seize us with your power and light, help us to protect
    all life,
to prepare for a better future,
for the coming of your Kingdom of justice, peace, love
    and beauty.
Praise be to you!
Amen.

Let's go!

In the inner journey of this book, we have explored the nether regions. We have clambered about in the darkness, slipped into the abyss of God's love and examined the geology of our soul. We have faced our demons and we have discovered breathtaking treasures and gems.

As it is time to return to the surface, we realise that there is no dichotomy between the world below and the world above, between spirituality and materiality, between the spiritual life and living in the world. It is one life and one world above and below. But we do realise that the quality of our life on the surface, its meaning, its very purpose, comes from below.

Closing prayer exercise

In a few moments of silence let us ponder these three questions:

- What has most delighted me in this book? *Give thanks…*

- What has most challenged me? *Note for yourself any resolve that emerges…*
- What is the next step I must take to move forwards in my spiritual journey?

Entrust your future to Christ…

Let us renew our commitment to keep on growing in God's love and to keep on seeking and searching for God's truth and justice.

Will you continue in the apostles' teaching and fellowship, in the breaking of bread, and in the prayers?
With the help of God, I will.

Will you persevere in resisting evil,
and, whenever you fall into sin, repent and return to the Lord?
With the help of God, I will.

Will you proclaim by word and example the good news of God in Christ?
With the help of God, I will.

Will you seek and serve Christ in all people, loving your neighbour as yourself?
With the help of God, I will.

Will you acknowledge Christ's authority over human society, by prayer for the world and its leaders, by defending the weak, and by seeking peace and justice?
With the help of God, I will.

May Christ dwell in your hearts through faith, that you may be rooted and grounded in love and bring forth the fruit of the Spirit.
Amen.[26]

Leabharlanna Poibli Chathair Bhaile Átha Cliath

Dublin City Public Libraries

Notes

Introduction

1 For a critique of the ascent model, see M. Miles, *The Image and Practice of Holiness* (SCM, 1989).

2 N.G. Cosby, *By Grace Transformed: Christianity for a new millennium* (Crossroad, 1998), p. 31.

3 Paul Tillich, *The Shaking of the Foundation* (Charles Scribner & Sons, 1955), ch. 7.

4 Richard Foster, *Celebration of Discipline* (Harper, 1988), p. 1.

5 P. Casaldaliga and J.M. Vigil, *The Spirituality of Liberation* (Tunbridge Wells, 1994), p. xxvii. See also Gustaf Gutiérrez, *We Drink from Our Own Wells* (SCM, 1984).

6 See M. Biddle, *The Tomb of Christ* (Sutton, 1999).

7 *Life of Constantine*, quoted in P.W.L. Walker, *Holy City, Holy Places?* (Oxford University Press, 1990), p. 186.

8 The Glittering Caves is one of very few locations in Tolkien's work that we can associate with a real place. They were inspired by the caves of Cheddar Gorge, in the southern English county of Somerset.

Chapter 1: Reading the geology of the soul

1 Capernaum is built of basalt rocks, for example.

2 M. Robert Mulholland Jr, *Invitation to a Journey: A road map for spiritual formation* (InterVarsity Press, 1993).

3 Quotations are from Clifton Wolters (tr.), *Richard Rolle: The fire of love* (Penguin, 1972), here Prologue. See also Rosamund Allen, (tr.), *Richard Rolle: English Writings*, Classics of Western Spirituality (Paulist Press, 1988). Rolle has been called 'the father of English literature'.

4 He writes about both physical sensations and psycho-auditory sensations, akin to locutions, as the hearing of a symphony of spiritual sounds or heavenly choirs that resonated somehow in his mind (ch. 15). He talks about experiencing sweetness of feeling in his body, and celebrates the emotions of wonder and joy, and of becoming 'intoxicated with sweetness ever more rare' (Wolters, *Richard Rolle*, p. 144). See Denis Reveney, *Language, Self and Love: Hermeneutics in the writings of Richard Rolle and the commentaries*

on the Song of Songs (University of Wales Press, 2001).

5   Letter 51, to Apostolic Nuncio to Tuscany.

6   Kieran Kavanaugh and Otilio Rodriguez (trs), *The Collected Works of St John of the Cross* (Institute of Carmelite Studies, 1991), pp. 641, 642.

7   Paschal Canon in Holy Transfiguration Monastery, *The Pentecostarion* (Holy Transfiguration Monastery, 1990), p. 29.

8   Benedicta Ward (tr.), *The Sayings of the Desert Fathers* (Cistercian Publications, Kalamazoo & A.R. Mowbray, 1975), p. 103.

9   E. Allison Peers (tr.), *St Teresa of Avila: Interior Castle* (Sheed & Ward, 1974), p. 37. See also E. Allison Peers, *Mother of Carmel: A portrait of St Teresa of Jesus* (Laing Press, 2003), p. 54. See also J.M. Cohen, *The Life of Teresa of Avila by Herself* (Penguin, 1957), chapter XI.

10   *Interior Castle*, IV:2:2, p. 37.

Chapter 2: Entering the cave of the heart

1   Ward, *Desert Fathers*, p. 139.

2   Richard M. Rice (tr.), *Lives of the Monks of Palestine by Cyril of Scythopolis* (Cistercian, 1991), p. 1.

3   All the quotations from Basil are from 'Letter 2' in Georges Barrois (tr.), *The Fathers Speak* (St Vladimir's Seminary Press, 1986).

4   Ward, *Sayings*, p. 131.

5   E. Allison Peers (tr.), *St Teresa of Avila: Interior Castle* (Sheed & Ward, 1974), pp. 1–2. For a recent translation, see Kieran Kavanaugh and Otilio Rodriguez (trs), *Teresa of Avila: The Interior Castle* (Paulist Press, 1979).

6   Rowan Williams, *Teresa of Avila* (Continuum, 1991), pp. 113, 114.

7   Carolyn Humphreys, *From Ash to Fire: A contemporary journey through the Interior Castle of Teresa of Avila* (New City Press, 1992), p. 80. See also Tessa Bielecki, *Teresa of Avila: An introduction to her life and writings* (Burns & Oates, 1994).

8   Peers, *Teresa*, p. 33.

9   It is the Indian tradition that first speaks of 'the cave of the heart'. See Abhishiktananda, *Hindu–Christian Meeting Point: Within the cave of the heart* (ISPCK, 1983). Abhishiktananda, *Saccidananda: A Christian approach to Advaitic experience* (ISPCK, 2007).

10   Libreria Editrice Vaticana, *Catechism of the Catholic Church* (Chapman, 1994), p. 545.

11   See Hans Walter Wolff, *Anthropology of the Old Testament* (SCM, 1974).

12 Kallistos Ware, *The Inner Kingdom* (St Vladimir's Seminary Press, 2000), p. 62.

13 Richard Rohr, *Everything Belongs* (Crossroad, 2003), p. 97.

14 George E.H. Palmer, Phillip Sherrard and Kallistos Ware (trs), *The Philokalia*, vol. 1 (Faber & Faber, 1979), p. 362.

15 Kallistos Ware, 'Ways of Prayer and Contemplation I: Eastern' in Bernard McGinn, John Meyendorff and Jacques Leclerq (eds), *Christian Spirituality: Origins to the twelfth century* (SCM, 1985), p. 401.

16 Attributed to Symeon the New Theologian, 'Three Methods of Attention and Prayer' in E. Kadloubovsky and George E.H. Palmer (eds), *Writings from the Philokalia* (Faber & Faber, 1977), p. 158.

17 John Meyendorff, *Byzantine Theology: Historical trends and doctrinal themes* (Mowbray, 1975), p. 77.

18 John Meyendorff, *St Gregory Palamas and Orthodox Spirituality* (St Vladimir's Seminary Press, 1974), p. 58.

19 Quoted in Andrew Louth, *Theology and Spirituality* (SLG Press, 5th edn, 2000), p. 4.

20 Richard Foster, *Prayer: Finding the heart's true home* (Hodder & Stoughton, 1992), p. 1.

21 Kieran Kavanaugh and Otilio Rodriguez (trs), *The Collected Works of St John of the Cross* (Institute of Carmelite Studies, 1991), pp. 673, 680–81.

22 See John Twisleton, *Using the Jesus Prayer: Steps to a simpler Christian life* (BRF, 2014).

Chapter 3: Plunging beneath the waters

1 The inscription is now in the Istanbul Museum.

2 James Roose-Evans, *The Inner Stage: Finding a center in prayer and ritual* (Cowley, 1990), p. 129.

3 Mischa Kudian (tr.), *Nerses Shnorhali: Jesus the Son* (Mashtots Press, 1986), p. 45.

4 Matthew Fox, *Wrestling with the Prophets* (Jeremy P. Tarcher, 2004).

5 David Anderson, 'God Is an Underground River', www.findingyoursoul.com/category/abundance.

6 Kieran Kavanaugh and Otilio Rodriguez (trs), *The Collected Works of St John of the Cross* (Institute of Carmelite Studies, 1991), p. 435.

7 Kavanaugh and Rodriguez, *Collected Works of St John*, pp. 58–59.

8 Gerhard von Rad, *Genesis* (SCM, 3rd rev. edn, 1972), p. 325.

9   For a different view see Claus Westermann, *Genesis 12—36: A commentary* (SPCK, 1985). Westermann sees this as an encounter with a river demon, and the divine elements as late additions. For a further reflection, see Andrew D. Mayes, *Spirituality of Struggle: Pathways to growth* (SPCK, 2002).

10 It evokes both the creation account of order emerging from the waters of chaos (Genesis 1) and the exodus story of liberation where foes were drowned in the waters of the Red Sea and where a barrier became a crossing place. It also recalls the Old Testament theme of dragons and demons lurking in the dark waters (cf. Job 41:1; Psalm 74:14).

11 Henri J.M. Nouwen, *Ministry and Spirituality* (Continuum, 1998), p. 161.

12 Walter Brueggemann, *Genesis: A Bible commentary for teaching and preaching* (John Knox Press, 1982), p. 271.

13 Andrew T. Lincoln, *The Gospel According to St John*, Black's New Testament Commentaries (Continuum, 2005), p. 397.

14 D. Moody Smith, *John* (Abingdon Press, 1999), p. 298.

15 Thomas L. Brodie, *The Gospel According to John: A literary and theological commentary* (Oxford University Press, 1997), p. 498.

16 William Temple, *Readings in St John's Gospel* (Macmillan, 1970).

17 C.K. Barrett, *A Commentary on the First Epistle to the Corinthians* (A & C Black, 1968), p. 75.

18 James W. Kinn, *The Spirit of Jesus in Scripture and Prayer* (Sheed & Ward, 2004), p. 14.

19 Quoted in Matthew Fox, *Illuminations of Hildegard of Bingen* (Bear & Co., 2002), p. 94.

20 See, for example, Alistair MacIntyre, *After Virtue: A study in moral theory* (Duckworth, 1985); Jean Porter, *The Recovery of Virtue* (SPCK, 1994); Christopher Cocksworth, *Wisdom: The Spirit's gift* (Grove, 2003).

21 David F. Ford, *The Shape of Living* (Fount, 1997), p. 72.

22 T.S. Eliot, 'Choruses from the Rock' in *Collected Poems 1909–1962* (Faber & Faber, 1974).

23 John Ziesler, *Paul's Letter to the Romans* (SCM, 1989), p. 227.

24 Roger Stronstad, *The Charismatic Theology of St Luke* (Hendrickson, 1984), p. 80.

25 Jürgen Moltmann, *The Spirit of Life: A universal affirmation* (Fortress Press, 2001), p. 283.

26 Moltmann, *Spirit of Life*, p. 285.

27 Gustaf Gutiérrez, *We Drink from Our Own Wells* (SCM, 1984), p. 37.

28 John V. Taylor, *The Go-Between God* (SCM, 1972), pp. 44–45.

29 Central Board of Finance of the Church of England, *Common Worship Initiation Services* (Church House Publishing, 1998).

30 From 'Parochial and Plain Sermons' viii in Erich Przywara (ed.), *The Heart of Newman* (Anthony Clarke, 1963).

Chapter 4: Carving out cisterns

1 Timothy Fry (ed.), *The Rule of St Benedict in English* (Liturgical Press, 1982), Prologue, p. 1.

2 David Robinson, *The Family Cloister: Benedictine wisdom for the home* (Crossroad, 2000).

3 Quentin R. Skrabec, *St Benedict's Rule for Business Success* (Purdue University Press, 2005).

4 Joan Chittister, *Wisdom Distilled from the Daily: Living the Rule of St Benedict today* (Harper, 1991), p. 7.

5 See Barry A. Harvey, *Another City: An ecclesiological primer for a post-Christian world* (Trinity Press International, 1999).

6 See the research in Yvonne Warren, *The Cracked Pot: The state of today's parish clergy* (Kevin Mayhew, 2002); for Roman Catholic research, see Dean R. Hoge, *The First Five Years of the Priesthood: A study of newly ordained Catholic priests* (Liturgical Press, 2002). For an earlier study, John A. Sanford, *Ministry Burnout* (Arthur James, 1982).

7 Esther de Waal, *Living with Contradiction: An introduction to Benedictine spirituality* (Canterbury Press, 1989).

8 Quoted in John Meyendorff, *St Gregory Palamas and Orthodox Spirituality* (St Vladimir's Seminary Press, 1974), p. 49.

9 Symeon reflects further on this in texts preserved in the *Philokalia*. It is published in four volumes: George E.H. Palmer, Phillip Sherrard and Kallistos Ware (trs), *The Philokalia: The complete text* (Faber & Faber, vol. 1 1979, vol. 2 1982, vol. 3 1986, vol. 4 1999).

10 Alexander Golitzin (tr.), *St Symeon the New Theologian: On the Mystical Life: Ethical discourses* (St Vladimir's Seminary Press, 1996).

11 Maximos the Confessor, 'Four Hundred Texts on Love' in Palmer, Sherrard and Ware, *Philokalia*, vol. 2, p. 69.

12 Maximos the Confessor, 'Texts on Love', p. 74.

Chapter 5: Tunnelling beneath the rock

1 Ali Qleibo, 'Palestinian Cave Culture: Underground cities and cave dwellings in the mountains of Hebron', *This Week in Palestine* (March 2011), www.palestine-family.net.

2 William A. Barry and William J. Connolly, *The Practice of Spiritual Direction* (Seabury Press, 1982), p. 67.

3 Mary E. Giles (tr.), *Francisco de Osuna: The Third Spiritual Alphabet* (Paulist Press, 1981), p. 39.

4 Giles, *Osuna*, p. 7.

5 Carolyn Gratton, *The Art of Spiritual Guidance* (Crossroad, 1992), p. 31.

6 Joseph Campbell, *Thou Art That: Transforming religious metaphor* (New World Library, 2013), p. 6.

7 Sandra M. Schneiders, 'Approaches to the Study of Christian Spirituality', in A. Holder (ed.), *The Blackwell Companion to Christian Spirituality* (Blackwell, 2005).

8 For a fuller exploration of language in spirituality see Andrew D. Mayes, *Learning the Language of the Soul* (Liturgical Press, 2016), to which this chapter is indebted.

9 'Ethical Discourses 7' in Alexander Golitzin (tr.), *St Symeon the New Theologian: On the Mystical Life* (St Vladimir's Seminary Press, 1996).

10 Kathleen Fischer, *Women at the Well: Feminist perspectives on spiritual direction* (SPCK, 1988), pp. 65–66.

11 Robert Moore and Douglas Gillette, *The King Within: Accessing the king in the male psyche* (Harper & Row, 1989), p. 33.

12 See Sherry Turkle, *Life on the Screen: Identity in the age of the Internet* (Simon & Schuster, 1997). See also Sara Savage, Sylvia Collins-Mayo, Bob Mayo, *Making Sense of Generation Y: The world view of 15–25 year olds* (Church House Publishing, 2006); Sylvia Collins-Mayo, Bob Mayo, Sally Nash, *The Faith of Generation Y* (Church House Publishing, 2010); Wendy Murray Zoba, *Generation 2K: What parents and others need to know about the millennials* (InterVarsity Press, 1999).

13 John Twisleton, *Using the Jesus Prayer: Steps to a simpler Christian life* (BRF, 2014).

Chapter 6: Plummeting into the abyss

1 Shimon Gibson, *The Final Days of Jesus: The archaeological evidence* (HarperOne, 2009).

2   Josephus, *War* 1:21:3.

3   Melvyn Matthews, *Both Alike to Thee: The retrieval of the mystical way* (SPCK, 2000).

4   Matthew Fox, *Wrestling with the Prophets* (Tarcher/Putnam, 1995), p. 13.

5   Jean Danielou, 'Introduction' in Herbert Musurillo (tr.), *From Glory to Glory: Texts from Gregory of Nyssa's mystical writings* (John Murray, 1962), p. 27.

6   Abraham J. Malherbe and Everett Ferguson (trs), *Gregory of Nyssa: The Life of Moses* (Paulist Press, 1978), p. 95.

7   Danielou, 'Introduction' in Musurillo, *From Glory*, p. 30.

8   Andrew Louth, *The Origins of the Christian Mystical Tradition* (Oxford University Press, 1981), p. 91. For a more cautious approach to mystical experience but celebrating the apophatic tradition in theology, see D. Turner, *The Darkness of God: Negativity in Christian mysticism* (Cambridge University Press, 1995).

9   'The Mystical Theology' 1 in Colm Luibheid (tr.), *Pseudo-Dionysius: The complete works* (Paulist Press, 1987), p. 135. See also Andrew Louth, *Denys the Aeropagite* (Continuum, 1989).

10   'Mystical Theology' in Luibheid, *Pseudo-Dionysius*, p. 139.

11   'Mystical Theology' 1:1 in Luibheid, *Pseudo-Dionysius*, p. 135.

12   See perspective in Bernard McGinn, *The Foundation of Mysticism,* vol. 1: *Origins to the fifth century* (SCM, 1991).

13   Ursula Fleming (ed.), *Meister Eckhart: The man from whom God hid nothing* (Collins/Fount, 1988), p. 90.

14   Matthew Fox (tr.), *Meditations with Meister Eckhart* (Bear & Co., 1983), p. 49.

15   Fox, *Eckhart*, p. 110.

16   Maria Shrady (tr.), *Johannes Tauler: Sermons* (Paulist Press, 1995), p. 90.

17   Johannes Tauler, 'Song of Bareness' quoted in Paul A. Dieṭrich, 'The Wilderness of God in Hadewijch and Meister Eckhart and His Circle' in Bernard McGinn (ed.), *Meister Eckhart and the Beguine Mystics* (Continuum, 1994), p. 42.

18   Colombo Hart (tr.), *Hadewijch: The Complete Works* (Paulist Press, 1980), p. 86.

19   Hart, *Hadewijch*, pp. 337, 345.

20   Paul Lachance (ed.), *Angela of Foligno: Passionate mystic of the double abyss* (New City Press, 2006), p. 28.

21   Lachance, *Angela of Foligno: Passionate mystic*, p. 73.

22 Lachance, *Angela of Foligno: Passionate mystic*, p. 79.
23 P. Lachance (tr.), *Angela of Foligno: Complete works* (Paulist Press, 1993), p. 206.
24 Lachance, *Angela of Foligno: Passionate mystic*, p. 30.
25 Rowan Williams, *The Wound of Knowledge* (Cowley, 1991), pp. 172, 173, 180.
26 See M. Basil Pennington, *Centering Prayer: Renewing an ancient Christian prayer form* (Doubleday, 1980); Thomas Keating, *Intimacy with God: An introduction to centering prayer* (Crossroad, 2009).

Chapter 7: Facing the dragons

1 Karl Rahner, 'The divided and enigmatic nature of humanity' in K. Lehmann, A. Raffelt and H.D. Egan (eds), *The Content of Faith: The best of Karl Rahner's theological writings* (Crossroad, 1992), p. 120.
2 Josephus, *Discourse to the Greeks Concerning Hades* 1.
3 In a memorable translation, the Living Bible gives us this episode too: 'At the place where the road passes some sheepfolds, Saul went into a cave to go to the bathroom, but as it happened, David and his men were hiding in the cave' (1 Samuel 24:3).
4 Origen, *Contra Celsus* 1:51.
5 Mother Mary and Kallistos Ware (trs), *The Festal Menaion* (Faber & Faber, 1969), p. 203.
6 Mary and Ware, *Menaion*, p. 205.
7 Mary and Ware, *Menaion*, p. 238.
8 From Wisdom 18:14–15.
9 Paul Tillich, *Systematic Theology: Part III* (SCM, 1978), pp. 175, 176.
10 Hugh Whybrew, *Risen with Christ* (SPCK, 2001), p. 28.
11 Aleksandr A. Bogolepov, *Orthodox Hymns of Christmas, Holy Week and Easter* (Russian Orthodox Theological Fund, 1965), p. 50.
12 Holy Transfiguration Monastery, *The Pentecostarion* (Holy Transfiguration Monastery, 1990), p. 34.
13 Ascent 2:1 in Kieran Kavanaugh and Otilio Rodriguez (trs), *The Collected Works of St John of the Cross* (Institute of Carmelite Studies, 1991), p. 120.
14 John Follent, 'Negative Experience and Christian Growth' in Peter Slattery (ed.), *St John of the Cross* (Alba House, 1994), p. 97.
15 Carl G. Jung, 'Psychology and Religion' in *Collected Works,* vol. 11: *Psychology and Religion: West and East* (Princeton University Press, 1970), p. 131.

16 See, for example, John Monbourquette, *How to Befriend Your Shadow: Welcoming your unloved side* (Darton, Longman & Todd, 2001).

17 Benedicta Ward (tr.), *The Sayings of the Desert Fathers: The alphabetical collection* (Cistercian, 1975), p. 87.

18 Ward, *Sayings*, p. 3.

19 See Samuel Rubenson, *The Letters of St Anthony: Monasticism and the making of a saint* (Fortress Press, 1995), p. 59.

20 'Letter Three' in Rubenson, *Letters*, p. 206.

21 Thomas Merton, *The Wisdom of the Desert* (Shambhala, 1960), pp. 4, 7.

22 For an exploration of liminality in the spiritual journey see Andrew D. Mayes, *Beyond the Edge: Spiritual transitions for adventurous souls* (SPCK, 2014). This chapter is indebted to Andrew D. Mayes, *Holy Land? Challenging questions from the biblical landscape* (SPCK, 2011).

23 Henri Nouwen, *The Way of the Heart* (Darton, Longman & Todd, 1987), pp. 27, 32.

24 This, and next quote from the Desert Fathers come from Ward, *Sayings*, pp. 95, 97.

25 Richard Rohr, *Dancing Standing Still: Healing the world from a place of prayer* (Paulist Press, 2015).

Chapter 8: Mining buried treasure

1 'Archaeology in Israel: Alexander the Great era cave treasure', www. jewishvirtuallibrary.org/jsource/Archaeology/cavetreasure2015. html. Israel is one of the world's centres for diamond cutting and polishing. Almost one quarter of its exports is diamonds—though the precious stones come from South Africa.

2 Sebastian Brock, *The Luminous Eye: The spiritual world vision of St Ephrem the Syrian* (Cistercian, 1992), 'Hymn on Faith' 32:2–3, 44.

3 From 'Hymn on Faith' 10 in Brock, *Luminous Eye*. The three extracts from St Ephrem are Copyright 1992 by Cistercian Publications and published by Liturgical Press.

4 'Hymn on Faith' 3 in Brock, *Luminous Eye*, p. 73.

5 'Hymn on the Church' 29 in Brock, *Luminous Eye*, p. 75.

6 Thomas J. Samuelian (tr.), *St Grigor Narekatsi: Speaking with God from the depths of the heart* (Vem Press, 2002); Mischa Kudian (tr.), *Nerses Shnorhali: Jesus the Son* (Mashtots Press, 1986).

7   Matthew the Poor, *Orthodox Prayer Life: The interior way* (St Vladimir's Seminary Press, 2003).

8   Br. Ramon, *Jacopone* (Collins/Flame, 1990), pp. 172, 181.

9   S. and E. Hughes (trs), *Jacopone da Todi: The Lauds* (Paulist Press, 1982). Jacopone is credited with being the author of the passiontide hymn *Stabat mater dolorosa* ('At the cross her station keeping').

10   James A. Wiseman (tr.), *John Ruusbroec: The Spiritual Espousals and other works* (Paulist Press, 1985), pp. 160, 161.

11   Wiseman, *Ruusbroec*, p. 180.

12   Kieran Kavanaugh and Otilio Rodriguez (trs), *Teresa of Avila: The Interior Castle* (Paulist Press, 1979), p. 35.

13   E. Allison Peers (tr.), *St Teresa of Avila: Interior Castle* (Sheed & Ward, 1974), pp. 6, 8.

14   Kavanaugh and Rodriguez, *Teresa of Avila*, p. 86.

15   Kavanaugh and Rodriguez, *Teresa of Avila*, p. 137.

16   Thomas Merton, *Conjectures of a Guilty Bystander* (Image, 1968).

17   Richard Rohr, *Immortal Diamond: the search for our true self* (SPCK, 2013), pp. 184, 185.

18   An idea explored by Jung in *Psychology and Alchemy, Collected Works of C.G. Jung*, vol. 12 (Princeton University Press, 1968).

19   Kavanaugh and Rodriguez, *Teresa of Avila*, p. 36.

Chapter 9: Calling from below

1   Dorothy Soelle, *The Inward Road and the Way Back* (Darton, Longman & Todd, 1978), p. 136.

2   Sang H. Lee, *From a Liminal Place: An Asian American theology* (Fortress Press, 2010), p. 47.

3   See Ernst Bammel and C.F.D. Moule (eds), *Jesus and the Politics of His Day* (Cambridge University Press, 1984).

4   Peter Walker, *Jesus and His World* (Lion, 2003), p. 30.

5   There is a scholarly debate about the nature of Jesus as prophet. Wright sees Jesus as an apocalyptic prophet who embodies the very presence of Israel's God; Sanders sees Jesus as one of a series of Jewish eschatological prophets. See Nicholas T. Wright, *Jesus and the Victory of God* (SPCK, 1996) and Ed p. Sanders, *The Historical Figure of Jesus* (Penguin, 1993).

6   This phrase derives from John Dominic Crossan, *Jesus: A revolutionary biography* (HarperCollins, 2009). See also John Dominic Crossan, *God and Empire: Jesus against Rome, then and now* (Harper, 2007).

7   Ronald J. Sider, *Rich Christians in an Age of Hunger: Moving from affluence to generosity* (Hodder & Stoughton, 1990).

8   See Stanley Hauerwas and William H. Willimon, *Resident Aliens* (Abingdon Press, 1989); Michael L. Buddle and Robert W. Brimlow (eds), *The Church as Counterculture* (State University of New York Press, 2000); Barry A. Harvey, *Another City: An ecclesiological primer for a post-Christian world* (Trinity Press International, 1999).

9   John Dear, *Jesus the Rebel: Bearer of God's peace and justice* (Sheed & Ward, 2000), p. 29. See also John Howard Yoder, *The Politics of Jesus* (Eerdmans, 1996) (Andrew D. Mayes, *Another Christ: Re-envisioning ministry* (SPCK, 2014), to which this section is indebted).

10 Pedro Casaldaliga and Jose M. Vigil, *The Spirituality of Liberation* (Burns & Oates, 1994), p. 103.

11 Justin Welby, Presidential Address to General Synod of the Church of England, 5 July 2013.

12 Jim Wallis, *The Soul of Politics* (Fount, 1994), pp. 38, 47.

13 Dorothy Soelle, *The Silent Cry: Mysticism and resistance* (Fortress Press, 2001). See also Dorothy Soelle, *The Window of Vulnerability: A political spirituality* (Fortress Press, 1990).

14 Kees Waaijman, *Spirituality: Forms, foundations, methods* (Peeters, 2002), p. 131.

15 Matthew Fox, *Original Blessing* (Bear and Co., 1987).

16 Soelle, *Silent Cry*, p. 90.

17 Soelle, *Silent Cry*, p. 93.

18 Soelle, *Silent Cry*, p. 89.

19 Soelle, *Silent Cry*, pp. 55, 56.

Chapter 10: Treading lightly

1   Matthew 6:33, my translation.

2   Plato, *Republic*, 518, quoted in Andrew Louth, *The Origins of the Christian Mystical Tradition* (Oxford University Press, 2007), p. 6.

3   John Walsh (ed.), *The Cloud of Unknowing* (Paulist Press, 1981), pp. 128, 131.

4   Philip Sheldrake, *Spirituality and History* (SPCK, 1991), p. 32.

5   See, for example, Archbishops' Council, *Mission-shaped Church* (Church House Publishing, 2004), p. 9.

6   'Spirituality in Higher Education: A national study of college students'. Search for meaning and purpose on www.spirituality.ucla.edu.

7   See John Ziesler, *Pauline Christianity* (Oxford University Press, 1990), p. 9.

8   This paragraph is indebted to an article by Michael Downey (ed.), *The New Dictionary of Catholic Spirituality* (Liturgical Press, 1993).

9   Quoted in Kees Waaijman, *Spirituality: Forms, foundations, methods* (Peeters, 2002), pp. 455–56.

10   Waaijman, *Spirituality*, p. 426.

11   Robert Warren, *Building Missionary Congregations: Towards a post-modern way of being church* (Church House Publishing, 1995).

12   Gordon Wakefield, *A Dictionary of Christian Spirituality* (SCM, 3rd edn, 1983), p. v.

13   Katherine M. Dyckman and L. Patrick Carroll, *Inviting the Mystic, Supporting the Prophet: An introduction to spiritual direction* (Paulist Press, 1981), p. 79.

14   Kenneth Leech, *The Eye of the Storm: Spiritual resources for the pursuit of justice* (Darton, Longman & Todd, 1992), p. 16.

15   Gerald W. Hughes, *God in All Things* (Hodder & Stoughton, 2003), ch. 1.

16   Robert M. Brown, *Spirituality and Liberation* (Spire, 1988).

17   For a recent exploration of garden imagery see Jennifer Rees Larcombe, *A Year's Journey with God* (Hodder & Stoughton, 2013).

18   Catherine Phillips (ed.), *Gerard Manley Hopkins: The major works* (Oxford University Press, 1986).

19   William Blake, from notebooks now known as *The Pickering Manuscript*.

20   Quoted in Fiona Bowie and Oliver Davies (eds), *Hildegard of Bingen: An anthology* (SPCK, 1990), p. 32.

21   Bowie and Davies, *Hildegard*, p. 32.

22   Martin Buber, *I and Thou* (Continuum International, 2004).

23   See, for example, Joseph M. Stoutzenberger and John D. Bohrer, *Praying with Francis of Assisi* (Saint Mary's Press, 1989).

24   Pope Francis, *Laudato Si': Care of Our Common Home*, paragraphs 217, 222.

25   We might begin by using the environmental toolkit via www.ecocongregation.org.

26   Archbishops' Council, *Christian Initiation* (Church House Publishing, 2001).